Summer Months Among the Alps

You are holding a reproduction of an original work that is in the public domain in the United States of America, and possibly other countries. You may freely copy and distribute this work as no entity (individual or corporate) has a copyright on the body of the work. This book may contain prior copyright references, and library stamps (as most of these works were scanned from library copies). These have been scanned and retained as part of the historical artifact.

This book may have occasional imperfections such as missing or blurred pages, poor pictures, errant marks, etc. that were either part of the original artifact, or were introduced by the scanning process. We believe this work is culturally important, and despite the imperfections, have elected to bring it back into print as part of our continuing commitment to the preservation of printed works worldwide. We appreciate your understanding of the imperfections in the preservation process, and hope you enjoy this valuable book.

LONDON:
Printed by SPOTTISWOODE & Co.
New-street Square.

MONT BLANC, FROM THE JARDIN.

THOMAS C. LINCH

MONT BLANC FROM THE FLEGÈRE.

SUMMER MONTHS

AMONG

THE ALPS:

WITH THE ASCENT OF MONTE ROSA.

BY

THOMAS W. HINCHLIFF,
OF LINCOLN'S INN, BARRISTER-AT-LAW.

LONDON:
LONGMAN, BROWN, GREEN, LONGMANS, & ROBERTS
1857.

The right of translation is reserved.

PREFACE.

AFTER spending three long vacations amidst the scenery of the Alps of Switzerland and Savoy, and making some expeditions in parts of the country little known and still less described, I was induced to hope that an account of such a combination of routes as would unite some of the more difficult enterprises among the high mountains with the walks that are within the reach of the less ambitious class of travellers, might perhaps be useful to those who have not yet seen these regions, as well as interesting to some who are already more or less acquainted with them.

With this view I have taken the last year's journey for my basis, and woven into the line such expeditions of former seasons as appeared likely to be most interesting and most worthy of being undertaken.

The materials have been collected from a complete journal which I kept in 1855, when Mr. W. Dundas accompanied me throughout nearly the whole of the journey, and from notes taken and letters written in 1856, when, with my brother and a friend, I visited the valleys and mountain passes to the south and east of Monte Rosa, in addition to retracing my steps over a great deal of old ground.

My object has been to describe, at some length, the grander and wilder features of the scenery, and some of the most interesting and exciting of the expeditions which I have had the good fortune to make successfully; passing over the less magnificent, but more beaten, routes with only such notice as is necessary to preserve the continuity of the march, and to enable a reader to follow my course without difficulty.

The surpassing grandeur of the neighbourhood of Zermatt and the Riffelberg, and the remembrance of the many happy days I have at various times spent there, coupled with the fact of its being infinitely less known than its great rival, Chamonix, have induced me to give the greatest prominence to that portion of the work which relates to the constellation of magnificent mountains, of which the many-peaked Monte Rosa is the chief star; and the pleasure of our ascent of its Höchste Spitze, or highest summit, under remarkably favourable circumstances of weather, forms the culminating point of my affection for this part of the Pennine Alps.

The Strahleck is probably the grandest pass in the Oberland, and the day's journey necessary to cross it gives a good insight into the mysteries of the Bernese Mer de Glace; and, though there is no difficulty in such passes as the Rawyl and Col de Checruit, I have described them carefully, in consequence of their being very little known, though highly worthy of the attention of travellers.

With respect to the illustrations, that of Monte Rosa is from a drawing very carefully made by my brother on the Riffelberg; the remainder are from drawings based upon our sketches taken on the spot, and finished by the kindness of friends at home. They are necessarily reduced to a small scale; yet such care has been bestowed upon them by Messrs. Day's lithographic artist, that I think I may venture to answer for their truthfulness.

It was impossible in a work of this size to give a map of sufficiently large dimensions to be useful in tracing a tour through the whole country; but I thought it would be advantageous to have a few small maps of the more important districts, where, without such assistance, it might be difficult for those unacquainted with the local geography to follow the routes indicated in the text.

They are taken in the main from the last edition of Keller's map, with the omission of many names of places unnecessary for the purposes of these pages, and the addition of some others and of a few routes not laid down in the original.

In the map of the Oberland mountains, some doubt may arise as to the accuracy of calling the glacier on the north side of the spur, running in a south-easterly direction from the Schreckhorn, by the name of the Lauteraar glacier. On this point Keller and Leuthold differ; the government survey is not yet continued quite far enough in this direction to the north to settle the question beyond a doubt; but, as far as we can judge from the way in which the surveyors have laid down the glaciers on each side of this spur, it would appear to be their intention to adopt Keller's view; and, as I have throughout used Keller as the chief standard, comparing him however with Leuthold, and with Studer whenever practicable, I have not hesitated to adhere to him in this instance also. At all events, it is a mere question of names. There is no doubt about the correctness of the position of the glaciers; and the route of the Strahleck Pass will, I think, be sufficiently clear after this explanation.

The remarks in the Appendix I submit with very great diffidence. I am far from being so presumptuous as to pretend to lay down rules as to what may or may not be properly considered an imperfect fluid; my only wish has been to show that, unless the objectors give us some strict definitions on the subject, they can hardly maintain the unsoundness of Professor Forbes's theory, which vindicates for a glacier the name, as well as the analogous phenomena, of an imperfect fluid; and I shall be truly glad if these remarks may lead to further discussion on the subject.

With regard to the supposed difficulties and dangers of expeditions above the level of perpetual snow, the greatness of which is by some persons estimated as sufficient to justify the charge of fool-hardiness levelled against those who encounter them willingly, I have throughout endeavoured to make it clear that, with tolerable training and proper precaution, nothing serious need be apprehended. At the same time, I think it only right to say that, without such preparations, grave difficulties may often be encountered; and, considering the uncertainty of weather on the high mountains, nothing short of the experience of many years can justify amateurs in undertaking expeditions of this nature without the assistance of local guides, who, by constant practice, acquire an almost instinctive power of extricating themselves from danger.

And if any one imagines that, because Mont Blanc has been very frequently ascended, the Alps in general are "done for," I would only imitate the example of the good curé of Saas, and point up to scores of glaciers and lofty peaks, untrodden by the foot of man, in the exploration of which much adventure, and probably no less valuable information, may yet be gleaned by those who like to start with "Excelsior" for their watchword.

CONTENTS.

CHAPTER I.

Freiburg. — The Höllenthal. — Schaffhausen. — Zurich. — The Rigi. — Lucerne. — Altdorf. — The Devil's Bridge. — Andermatt. — Hospenthal   .   .   .   .   Pp. 1—19

CHAP. II.

The Furka. — View of the Finsteraarhorn. — Glacier of the Rhone. — The Grimsel. — The Unteraar Glacier. — Falls of Handeck. — Reichenbach. — Rosenlaui. — Sunrise on the Faulhorn. — Grindelwald. — The Wengern Alp. — Interlaken   .   .   .   .   .   .   20—35

CHAP. III.

Passage of the Strahleck from the Grimsel to Grindelwald. — Crossing the Glacier. — "Das ist der Mond." — Sleep in the Hut. — A portable Wine-cellar. — Precipitous Ascent. — View from the Summit. — Descent to Grindelwald by the Lower Glacier   .   .   .   .   .   .   36—54

CHAP. IV.

Interlaken. — Kandersteg. — The Œschinen See. — Schwarenbach. — An old Friend. — Ascent of the Great Altels. — Singular Glacier. — Adventure on the Summit. — Cloudy Weather. — The Gemmi. — Leukerbad. — The Ladders
Pp. 55—81

CHAP. V.

The Baths of Leuk. — Visp. — Effects of the Earthquake. — St. Nicolaus. — A Race. — Zermatt. — The Schwartzen See. — The Hörnli. — Magnificent View. — The Theodule and Gorner Glaciers. — Hôtel du Riffel. — Preparations for Monte Rosa - - - - - 82—102

CHAP. VI.

An early Start. — A German Volunteer. — The first Rocks. — "Look at Mont Blanc!" — The old Route. — Severe Cold. — A difficult Crest. — Halt among the Rocks. — The last Obstacle. — Astonishing View from the Summit. — A trifling Accident. — Return to the Riffel - - 103—143

CHAP. VII.

Attempt to cross the Weiss Thor. — Dangerous Snow. — Bad Weather. — An awkward Situation. — The St. Theodule Pass, or Matterjoch. — A fast Walk to Chatillon. — Ascent of the Cima di Jazzi. — Crevasse in the Nevé. — Effect of Clouds. — Symptoms of Winter - - - 144—159

CHAP. VIII.

Farewell to the Riffel. — Stalden. — The Valley of Saas. — M. Imseng, the Mountaineering Curé. — The Allelein Glacier.—Pass of the Monte Moro to Macugnaga.—Lochmatter "at Home."—The Val d'Anzasca.—Ponte Grande.—Feriolo. —Lago Maggiore - - - - Pp. 160—177

CHAP. IX.

Arona. — The Isola Bella.—Lago d'Orta. — Pella to Varallo.— A Pilgrimage to the Monte Sacro. — A Village Theatre. — Val Sesia. — Pass of the Val Dobbia. — Gressonay. — The Lys Glacier and the Col d'Ollen. — Brusson. — Grapes and Walnuts. — Chatillon. — Aosta - - - 178—196

CHAP. X.

Stormy Weather on the St. Bernard. — Col Fenêtre and Col Ferrex. — Courmayeur. — The Proments.—Col de Checruit. — Col de la Seigne. — Col des Fours. — A Party lost. — Contamines.—Col de Voza.—The new Route to the Summit of Mont Blanc. — Les Ouches. — Chamonix - 197—217

CHAP. XI.

The Mer de Glace. — Expedition to the Jardin. — Chamonix Guides. — The Glacier de Talèfre. — The Brevent. — Jean Tairraz. —The Pierre de l'Échelle. —Excursion to the Glaciers at the Foot of the Aiguilles. — A Discovery. — Return to Chamonix - - - - - 218—237

CHAP. XII.

Start for the Buet. — Argentière. — A new Route. — View from the Summit. — A singular Line of Descent. — Pierre de Berar. — Glacier des Bossons. — Montanvert and the Mauvais Pas. — An American on Foot. — Wonderful Effect of Moonlight - - - - Pp. 238—257

CHAP. XIII.

Departure from Chamonix.—The Col de Balme.—Martigny.— An enthusiastic Engineer.— Lombard Sportsmen. — Sion. — Ayent.— Passage of the Rawyl.—Singular Cascades.— The Wildstrubel. — Beauties of the Simmenthal. — Ander Lenk
258—277

CHAP. XIV.

The Ober Simmenthal.— A hospitable Landlord.—The Sieben Brunnen. — The Räzli Glacier. — Long Walk down the Valley.—Boltigen.—Erlenbach.—An importunate Voiturier. — A Race into Thun.— Farewell Sunset on the Oberland Mountains - - - - - 278—288

CHAP. XV.

Choice of a Route.—Pleasures of a Second Visit.—The Outfit. — Guides. — Remarks on Fatigue. — Tales of Suffering. — Mountain Sickness. — Want of Food. — The Land of Freedom. — Alpine Scenery in general. — To say he " did it "
289—302

APPENDIX.

Remarks upon certain Observations with regard to the Nature and Motion of Glaciers - - - - 303—312

LIST OF ILLUSTRATIONS.

MAPS.

The Oberland Mountains . . .	to face p.	21
Monte Rosa and the Mountains around Zermatt	. ,,	85
Mont Blanc and the Surrounding Country .	. ,,	197

PLATES.

Monte Rosa, from the Riffelberg . .	. *Frontispiece*	
The Wetterhorn	to face p.	31
The Matterhorn	. ,,	90
The Wildstrubel and Räzli Glacier . .	. ,,	276

SUMMER MONTHS AMONG THE ALPS.

CHAPTER I.

Freiburg.—The Höllenthal.—Schaffhausen.—Zurich.—The Rigi.—Lucerne.—Altdorf.—The Devil's Bridge.—Andermatt.—Hospenthal.

EARLY in August 1856, we arrived at Freiburg, in Breisgau, with the view of entering Switzerland by way of Schaffhausen. We had listened to the silvery chimes of Antwerp, had been made aware of the many odours of Cologne, studied the fearful legends of the Rhine castles, and seen the glories of a sunset from the terrace-walk of Heidelberg. Our next step was to be a journey through the Black Forest and Höllenthal, instead of continuing the line of railway to Basle.

Though Heidelberg and Baden-Baden in one direction, and Basle in the other, are continually thronged with tourists, Freiburg is as yet happy in complete exemption from over-crowding and confusion. Few people seem to think of staying there, because there is nothing particularly fashionable in it, and thousands pass by without attempting to see anything more than a distant view of the cathedral spire from the window of the railway carriage. We only found about half-a-dozen visitors in the Zahringer Hof, the principal hotel; and yet Freiburg is an exceedingly interesting place in itself, in addition to being the key of what may be considered the most satisfactory route to Switzerland. In the evening we enjoyed ourselves in examining the wonderful beauties of the cathedral. The lofty spire is entirely composed of open stonework, through the carved interstices of which the light shines from the further side, and the structure looks so airy, that it is difficult to believe the material to be stone and not cast iron.

The colours of the glass in every window appeared to be richer and more glowing than any I had ever seen, and shed such a charming "dim religious light" through the interior, that we lingered there until the officials began to lock up the church for the night; but early in the morning we had a better opportunity of examining closely the perfect workmanship and exquisite tracery which adorn the whole building, and make it a marvel of art.

After breakfast we started by the diligence towards Schaffhausen, and were delighted to find that the beauty of the country we travelled over was even greater than we had anticipated. There being no regular banquette, we secured the only seats on the roof; and, though the heat and dust were excessive, we felt that we had no reason to envy the inside passengers, who could see but little of the surrounding scenery.

An ever-varying road twisted among undulating lofty hills covered with splendid wood from base to crown, where their bright green foliage contrasted itself with the deep blue of the sky. Sometimes the way led through a mere gorge, like the Via Mala, where vast precipitous rocks pressed closely on each side, out of many a cleft in which waved some mountain ash or dark pine, the delicious scent of the latter perfuming the whole air as we swept past almost within reach of their lower branches. Picturesque trains of timber-waggons, laden with their splendid stems, passed us on their way to the Rhine, which is ever ready to receive these denizens of the

Black Forest, and float them away in huge rafts, to be tortured into every variety of form for the convenience of mankind; and at many a charming corner by the side of the rushing mountain torrent, were saw-mills to dissect them on the spot, by means of very simple but effective machinery which is worked by water-power.

Soon after passing the Titi See, a beautiful little lake something like one of those in Cumberland, we had a very long pull uphill, where the sides of the road were covered with wild fruits and flowers; and looking back from the summit, we enjoyed a view across the lake, lying almost at our feet in the foreground, the beauty and charm of which could hardly be effaced by all the subsequent scenery of Switzerland.

We did not arrive at Schaffhausen until too late in the evening to see the Rheinfall, though we heard its roar very distinctly before we came to the Hotel Weber; but on the following morning we devoted several hours to this far-famed sight.

So much has been said of the falls of the Rhine at Schaffhausen, that my first feeling, on seeing them, was rather one of disappointment than otherwise. The impression conveyed was that of a tremendous rapid, instead of a waterfall; but the more I looked at the scene, the more aware I became of its grandeur. A singular contrast to this exhibition of nature's force is now seen in the shape of a railway bridge — one of the triumphs of human ingenuity. The river is at this part very wide; but close to the falls, just above where the whirling waters take their final rush, the railway to Basle is being carried across it, to dive through a tunnel under the very walls and gardens of the château from which the falls are seen.

The people of Switzerland are seldom blind to the great advantages of water-power, and all the way from the town to the falls, the bank of the river is dotted with busy factories, both great and small; and the rushing Rhine does all the work of the place, from sawing timber, down to blowing the blacksmiths' bellows.

In the afternoon we found a diligence going as far as Winterthur, where a train was waiting to take us on to Zurich. From some mismanagement, there was a grand scene of confusion at the station, and it was not till after a sharp struggle, aggravated by the heat of the weather, that we got our luggage upon the roof of an omnibus, and soon found ourselves established at the Hôtel Baur du Lac, with our windows looking out upon the bright blue waters of the Lake of Zurich, and the distant outlines of the mountain land.

When the burning glare of the day had departed, and the long evening shadows began to steal gently over the still surface of the lake, a little crowd of boats started from the shore with parties of bathers, whose merry laughter rang far across the water amid surrounding silence. The forest-clad hills on the western side grew more and more sombre, and darkness would soon embrace the lower world, but far away the rosy tinge still lingered on the snow-capped summits of the Glärnisch and its brethren. This had been my first glimpse of the mountains in 1854, and I always feel peculiar delight in reflecting on the feelings of wonder and excitement then first suggested to me by it.

We spent a great part of the following day in an expedition to the Utliberg, the summit of which may be reached in less than two hours, walking or riding. Leaving Zurich, the path takes a westerly direction, gradually ascending among orchards and meadows to the base of a steep hill covered with wood and ornamented with a vast variety of wild flowers, which must make it a perfect garden in the early summer. A short scramble over the edge brought us to the open summit, where a house has been erected for the refreshment of visitors. It appears to be far more frequented by Swiss than strangers, and, as it was Sunday afternoon, we found a large party of them seated at a long table in front of the house. Many of them appeared to be acquainted with each other, and, forming themselves in order, sang national songs and choruses in capital style, several of which, being highly patriotic, were received with a heartfelt enthusiasm worthy of a free people.

The view from this eminence is perfectly lovely, and, of course, far more extensive than that from Zurich. It commands the whole ridge which runs along the western side of the lake. The left of the picture includes the greater part of the lake itself, studded with the white sails of numberless boats, the picturesque town, and the vine-clad hills beyond; while on the right the eye ranges over an immense extent of undulating country to the great peaks around the Jungfrau, at a distance of about sixty miles. No more charming spot can be found for a preliminary glimpse of the wonders of the mountain district—the Promised Land of the pedestrian in Switzerland; and no one who can spare time for it should avoid making the experiment. We had some difficulty in tearing ourselves away so as to be in time for M. Baur's *table-d'hôte*, where we were fortunate enough to meet some English acquaintances.

The next morning we left in the steamboat for Horgen, after carefully packing our knapsacks, and sending away in a portmanteau the remainder of our effects which had been deemed necessary for respectability in the cities of Germany.

Arriving at Horgen, we shouldered our burdens, and set out for a short walk of three hours to Zug, great part of the road being among the fir-woods, and giving many a charming peep of the lake and surrounding country. It was, however, exceedingly hot, and, before getting over half our walk, both my companions, who were new to the work, declared that they would never more carry knapsacks unless the weather became cooler. Next day, however, the heat was, if possible, still greater as we crossed the lake of Zug to Imensee, and walked over to Küssnacht. A boy carried the knapsacks refused by their owners, and, after depositing them in the little inn, we prepared to ascend the Rigi, intending to return to Küssnacht in the evening. I had slept on the summit before; and, glorious as is the effect of the sunset seen from it, the bustle and confusion of this elevated human hive in the height of the season are so great that I had no objection to the proposed modification.

The amusement of the morning scene is, however, almost enough to compensate for the noise and confusion of the night. A little before sunrise the dreadful horn is sounded, and out rush some 150 people in every variety of incompleteness of toilet; some of them, in spite of all rules and regulations to the contrary, insisting on wearing their red-edged blankets, and stalking about the bleak summit with all the independence of so many New Zealand chiefs: some, however, lazier than the rest, hug themselves in the knowledge that their windows command the Oberland mountains, and are quite content to see what they can of the view without taking the trouble of getting out of bed for it.

On the present occasion the number of visitors was small, and the animated excitement much less than usual. Huge dark clouds had been for some hours collecting over the great mountains; flashes of lightning, accompanied by tremendous echoing rolls of thunder, frightened many into the house, and a few heavy drops of rain completed the rout very effectually. Presently the whole of the mountains to the south and west became invisible in the murky storm-cloud which came rapidly towards us, driving over the lofty summits like an army of demons maintaining a fire of artillery along the line of their advance. It was a remarkably grand sight to watch the approach of such a storm over a boundless vista of mountains; and the awful gloom of this side of the panorama contrasted strangely with the smiling beauty of all within the eastern half of the horizon, where the sun was still shining on the placid waters of the lake of Zug, and upon a thousand woods and valleys, all glowing with loveliness and unshaded by the western storm.

The heaviest part of the clouds, however, did not quite reach our position, but, owing to a change of wind, turned off towards the Rigi Scheideck; and as soon as the rain ceased we descended again to Küssnacht. The earth had as yet been only partially cooled; but in the night another storm burst over our heads with great severity, accompanied by such a deluge of rain as to make dust an impossibility for a week to come. As usual on these occasions, the bells of the village church began ringing violently, as soon as the ringers could be brought from their beds; and, as the church and the inn are close together, the uproar was for some hours tremendous. At length, however, the storm growled sulkily away in the distance, and in the morning the cooling effect of it upon the air and ground was very perceptible.

On arriving at Lucerne about noon, we again found the heat excessive; but happening to meet some English friends, we took them to see the famous rock-hewn lion sacred to the memory of the Swiss Guards who fell in Paris during the Great Revolution. It is a grand work, and stands in a very fine situation; but the good people of Lucerne have had the bad taste to allow its effect to be impaired by the erection of a shop, immediately in front of it, for the sale of wooden souvenirs and all the usual variety of temptations for visitors with full purses.

Thence we found a pretty walk through orchards at the back of the ancient wall, which brought us out on the bank of the swift-flowing Reuss at the other side of the town. Lounging on one of the singular old covered bridges, with the clear blue river rushing under our feet, we met a young Russian physician with whom we had formerly travelled in Baden; and, as he spoke English nearly as well as his own language, we had a long and interesting conversation on the effects of the late war, which he thought had taught his countrymen a useful lesson,— that they must not expect to stand any longer upon a footing of barbarism, but must make it their endeavour to compete with other nations in the cause of peace, progress, and civilization.

In the afternoon of the next day we went on board the fussy little steamer that was to carry us down the lake to Fluelen. On the evening before, another thunderstorm had set all the neighbouring bells in motion; and, as the picturesque outline of Mont Pilatus flashed in the lightning of the storm which raved about its hoary sides, one might imagine that the troubled spirit of Pontius Pilate himself was struggling to get free from the overpowering grasp which is said to hold it there in a rocky prison.

Nothing, however, could be more calm and tranquil than the Lake of Lucerne as we moved over its deep blue waters: the dark woods and noble mountains which surround it were all perfectly reflected in the watery mirror which rivalled even the heaven above in purity of colour. Turn after turn in its ever-winding course constantly revealed some new charm; some fresh inlet bathing the feet of pine-clad rocks, or more distant view of a village imbedded in green woods and meadows, with towering hills stretching away beyond till terminated in summits of snow; the whole forming a combination of scenery which, I must think, places the beauty of the Lake of Lucerne above that of any other which I have seen, not even excepting the Lago Maggiore.

Having no intention of sleeping at that nasty little place, Fluelen, where the steam-boat journey comes to an end, we walked on at once to Altdorf, about two miles further. In the old-fashioned village where Gessler's hat was scorned by William Tell, we found very comfortable quarters in the inn, where I was recognised by the people of the house as an old acquaintance. We strolled down towards the river in the evening, but the heat was so stifling in this neighbourhood, enclosed as it is by lofty hills, that we were soon glad to return and shut ourselves up in the house.

On returning from our walk we found the *salle à manger* in the possession of about half a dozen boys of ten or twelve years old, and before I had time to observe their faces, I was pounced upon by several of them and claimed as an old friend. I at once remembered them, as they had, in the year before, walked over the Wengern Alp to Grindelwald with Dundas and myself. They were pupils of M. Müller, who keeps a famous school near Berne, and during the summer holidays, when most of his boys go home, he always takes the remainder into the country for a pedestrian excursion. Each carried his little knapsack; and as they went running and jumping over the hills and bringing M. Müller the flowers they gathered, or making wreaths of rhododendrons for their hats, I thought I had never seen such happy, independent, and, at the same time, gentlemanly fellows. They now gathered around me, and talked about what we had seen together last year, and what they had since been doing, and all were in active conversation when M. Müller himself walked into the room, and I was very glad to have another evening with a man of high intelligence, who is completely acquainted with everything relating to the country. Some of his boys were English and one French; and the fondness which they all showed for each other, as well as for himself, spoke volumes in favour of his happy management of them.

In the morning we were obliged to part, as our routes lay in opposite directions: they were going to Lucerne, while we had ordered a carriage to take us along the St. Gothard road to Hospenthal. The horses were soon ready, and we started at a good pace, which was kept up pretty well till we arrived at Amsteg. Here we had to wait an hour; and, strolling out to the bridge, we were accosted by a steady, good-tempered fellow, who was very anxious to accompany us in the character of guide. I was perfectly acquainted with the way to Grimsel and Interlaken; but two knapsacks had to be carried, and as he offered to do this for six francs a day, we agreed to take him as porter, though there was no need of a guide. When the horses were ready, he jumped up on the front seat in a state of great delight and satisfaction.

There had been a fête in one of the villages on our road, and for many miles we were continually passing groups of peasants in all their holiday finery; picturesque as they were, however, it must be confessed that personal beauty formed no part of their attractions; all the *poudre de riz,* and all the silks and crinoline of Paris would not have made more than two out of a hundred of the women passably good-looking. Our guide, Johann Zurfluhr, proved a very agreeable companion, and, as a great part of the road from Amsteg was so steep that we walked on in front of the carriage, we had a good deal of conversation with him. It became steeper than ever as we approached Wasen, a curious little village perched up at a considerable height above the valley. From this point a very interesting walk over the Susten Pass, at the foot of the magnificent Titlis, may be followed to Meyringen in the Hasli Thal, by those who wish to avoid the Furka.

After leaving Wasen the road becomes wilder with every mile, savage rocky hills rising close above it on both sides, and at length, after passing through a tunneled gallery, to protect it from falling avalanches, another turn brings the traveller to the far-famed Devil's Bridge. This is a single ancient arch thrown across the furious stream of the Reuss, just below a point where it rushes down among savage and tremendous rocks, here and there ornamented with small bushes, waving to and fro in the hurricane of wind and spray brought down with the water. Some sixty years ago French and Austrians fought for life upon this narrow bridge without even a parapet to save the vanquished from falling headlong into the torrent, a hundred feet beneath. Anything more dreadful than such a scene could hardly be imagined, the only advantage being that the shrieks of the dying must have been stifled by the roar of the waterfall!

The old arch is now, however, only a relic of a bygone time : a solid and handsome bridge has of late years been carried across the river just above the old one, and thousands of travellers pass without any risk beyond a slight damping from the wild spray which drives past them like a cloud.

A little higher up the road is carried through

another gallery, at the end of which a startling change of scene breaks upon the eye: in a moment the bare rugged rocks have ceased, and a broad plain of rich green pasture, commencing at our very feet, fills up the whole space to the slopes of the St. Gothard mountains, whose snowy crests tower far on high, over the white buildings of Andermatt and Hospenthal.

In 1854, I spent a week, instead of a day, in getting from Altdorf to Andermatt, by a route which is full of interest, and well worth following when time is not an object. We began by walking over the Klausen Pass to the baths of Stachelberg, a charming village in the Lint Thal, from which there is a splendid view of the Tödi and neighbouring mountains. Thence we went to Glarus and Wasen at the extremity of the noble Lake of Wallenstadt; a steamer took us to Wallenstadt, and we then walked to Sargans and Ragatz. On the way we had an opportunity of observing what has long been a matter of anxious speculation among the engineering world. Between Ragatz and Sargans, the Rhine passes over a flat country, and then takes a sudden bend to the right. The difference of level is so slight between its present course and the line of road to Wallenstadt, which would be its natural direction, that an excessive rising of the water would soon divert the course of the river, and send it to the Lake of Wallenstadt, destroying everything in its way, and probably seriously changing the level of the Lake of Zurich.

We spent the next day in visiting the wonderful Old Baths of Pfeffers, where patients used formerly to be let down by a rope and stewed in a cave of hot water in the depths of a dark and dismal gorge, with scarcely a ray of daylight through the narrow opening, hundreds of feet over the bed of a rushing river. In these days, however, of everything-made-easy, the hot water of the spring is brought down through wooden pipes to the great Bad-Haus at Ragatz, a distance of about three miles, losing none of its efficacy excepting a portion of the caloric.

On the day after, we went to Coire and Reichenbach, devoting several hours to examining the former place, which is one of the most singular old towns to be seen. The principal attraction is a most curious old church in honour of St. Lucius, who is said to have been an early British saint: the pillars are ornamented with very grotesque, full-length figures instead of the quaint heads of the later Gothic architecture, and the crypt is declared to be as old as the sixth century.

Reichenbach is beautifully situated at the junction of the Hinter Rhein and Vorder Rhein, and is celebrated for the residence of Louis-Philippe, when a youthful exile. Thence we saw the wonders of the Via Mala on the Splügen road, and returning to Reichenbach, followed the course of the Vorder Rhein to Dissentis and the Ober Alp, over which we descended to Andermatt. As we crossed the Furka to the Grimsel immediately afterwards, we had the satisfaction of seeing the principal source of the Rhine on one day, and that of the Rhone on the next. What a variety of thoughts and historical reflections crowd upon the mind as we follow in imagination the course of these two mighty rivers from their mountain homes to the German Ocean and the Mediterranean!

Our present intention was to hasten to the Oberland, with the view of arriving as early as possible in the neighbourhood of Monte Rosa; and so, after reaching Hospenthal, and enjoying our supper in that dirty village, which has evidently borrowed much from the Italian filth on the South of the pass, Zurfluhr was ordered to be ready for an early start to the Furka, and we had a capital night's rest preparatory to the mountains.

CHAP. II.

The Furka. — View of the Finsteraarhorn. — Glacier of the Rhone and the Grimsel. — The Unteraar Glacier.— Falls of Handeck. — Reichenbach. — Rosenlaui. — Sunrise on the Faulhorn.— Grindelwald.— The Wengern Alp.— Interlaken.

ABOUT 7 o'clock in the morning, with perfectly fine weather, we started from Hospenthal, and arrived at the house on the Furka in a little under four hours. This ascent must be allowed to be one of the dreariest in the country, but it is atoned for by the view at the top of the pass, and there is no better route for entering the Oberland from the moment when this first height is attained. The want of variety in the scenery from Hospenthal has, no doubt, made the ascent wearisome to many of those who have tried it; but let none be discouraged: no one can fail to be completely recompensed for his fatigue, when he sees, for the first time, the monarch of the Oberland, the tremendous Finsteraarhorn. A moment before all was dulness, but a step further has placed us on the summit of

the Furka; and exactly in front of us, at a distance of only fifteen miles, this magnificent mountain lifts its snow-wreathed precipices into the deep blue sky. The inferior mountains on each side of the pass form a sort of frame for the picture of their dread lord, and close in the view so completely, that no other prominent feature in the Oberland is visible from this point; nothing withdraws the attention from the solitary grandeur of the Finsteraarhorn, and the dependent spurs which form the abutments of the central peak. This distance is about the same as that of Mont Blanc when seen from the Buet, and appears to me, as nearly as possible, the *juste milieu* for the observation of a mountain of the highest class: when seen from nearer points, such a mountain can scarcely be comprehended by the eye, while, on the other hand, beautiful as are the snowy summits at immense distances, it must be admitted that their perfection is somewhat impaired by indistinctness of detail.

Close on our right, green sloping pastures lead the eye up towards the snowy crest of the Galenstok; and, as we were talking to the proprietor of the little inn, we were informed that an English gentleman had ascended to its summit on the day before. This turned out upon inquiry to be a friend of mine, and in a few minutes he walked into the room with his brother, to my great satisfaction. We talked about the Galenstok, and it appeared he had ascended from the house on the Furka with two of its domestics as guides. Nothing, however, was known of the route to be taken, and they had five hours of real hard work to reach the top. He was of opinion, after seeing the whole aspect of the mountain from above, that they might have ascended with much greater ease by a different route. He had also attempted the Finsteraarhorn a few weeks earlier, and arrived at a very great elevation, when, finding that if they proceeded further they should have to sleep on the bare mountain without any extra clothes, they were reluctantly compelled to return to the Aeggischhorn. He was on his way to make a second attempt when we saw him; so it was agreed, that after our luncheon, we should all walk down to the foot of the Rhone glacier together, and there diverge in our different directions.

With the addition of some other acquaintances, who were also bound for the Grimsel, we formed a large party as we descended the path which winds round the shoulder of a mountain towards the glacier. For the especial benefit of some of the party, who had never seen a glacier before, we left the path and took to the ice; and after wandering amongst the crevasses a little, to admire the wonders of these deep blue caverns, and hear the rushing of waters through their subglacial channels, we struck out a course towards the opposite side, and crossed the glacier successfully, a little above the cave from which the infant Rhone takes its first bound out of the icy depths. Half a mile below this our routes diverged: my Galenstok friend and his brother followed the course of the Rhone through the gorge which leads into the open valley near Obergestelen, and we began to climb the flowery side of the Meienwand. One of our party started before the rest, but the heat was so great, that we found him quite exhausted, and lying at full length in the shade of a large stone. We sat down with him for a time, for all felt the heat exceedingly in the climb up this very steep hill side, and then we set out again together, and arrived at last near the Dead Man's Lake, at the foot of the Sidelhorn. This lonely spot, once used for an extempore burying place, after a sanguinary skirmish between the French and Austrians, is the very perfection of desolation: there is nothing in sight to mark the hand of man, except the line of weather-beaten whitened posts, set up to indicate the direction of the pass in the snows of winter. Near this point the footpath joins the wider track, which connects the Grimsel with the head of the Rhone valley: this has been carefully constructed, and leads with a tortuous course among and over the rocks, down to the bank of the gloomy little lake, which almost washes against the walls of the Grimsel Hospice. We arrived a little before 4 o'clock at the end of our day's journey, hot enough to justify the step, taken by most of the party, of plunging into the crystal water of the snow-fed lake.

The next afternoon we started for a walk up the Unteraar glacier, with the intention of, at all events, getting as far as the hut which is used as a sleeping place by most of those who cross the Strahleck Pass to Grindelwald. We got over the tedious collection of stones and *débris* which covers the foot of the glacier, and had walked nearly three hours from the Grimsel, when, just as we were thinking of crossing over to the right, to climb the cliffs at the foot of the hut, the clouds, which had for some time assumed a threatening appearance, suddenly dropped, and a huge mass of them, driving towards us from the Finsteraarhorn, poured down a deluge of rain and hail. Fortunately, we were not far from a very large glacier table; it was a huge rock balanced on a pedestal of ice high enough to admit of our all creeping under it for shelter. A stream of water had furrowed a course for itself in the ice at its base, and we were obliged to stand with one foot on each side of this, and endeavour to keep ourselves warm by cutting steps in the steep bank of the pedestal, so as to get a higher place for standing on, as the water rose rapidly in its trench. A very cold wind accompanied the storm, and made our position far from pleasant; and presently came a flash of lightning, apparently in the middle of our little party, with an instantaneous clap of thunder, sounding like a large gun fired close to our ears: the effect was startling; but in a few seconds our attention was fixed by the roaring echoes of the thunder against the tremendous mountains which completely surrounded us. This was followed by many more bursts, none of which, however, was so dangerously near; and after waiting a long half hour in our icy prison, we sallied out to walk through a rain which, though not so heavy as before, was quite enough to give us a thorough soaking before our arrival at the Hospice.

The Grimsel is certainly a wonderful place; situated at the bottom of a sort of huge crater, the sides of which are utterly savage mountains, composed of barren rocks which cannot even support a single pine tree, and afford only scanty food for a herd of goats, it looks as if it must be completely buried in the winter snows. Enormous avalanches fall against it every spring, sometimes covering everything to the depth of thirty or forty feet; and, in spite of walls four feet thick, and furnished with outside iron shutters, the two men who stay here when the *voyageurs* are snugly quartered in their distant homes can tell you that the snow sometimes shakes the house to its foundations. This year there was unusually little snow throughout the country; and many places which, in 1855, I saw covered by immense beds of it in the month of August were now entirely free, and garnished with abundance of mountain flowers.

Next morning the weather still continued bad, but we made up our minds to go on, and make the best of it. Half an hour after we started the rain thickened unpleasantly, and we attempted to get shelter under a projecting rock, but being far too wet already to make standing at all agreeable, we pushed on for the Handeck, consoling ourselves with the reflection that from the furious rushing of the river Aar at our side, we should at all events see the celebrated waterfall in great perfection. Nor were we disappointed in our expectation; the water was roaring down its leap of 250 feet in a most magnificent frenzy, while the trees which cling to its rocky sides swayed to and fro in the violence of the hurricane which it brought down with it: even the stream, which falls into the main cascade at right angles, and always forms a beautiful feature in the scene, was now swollen into a raging torrent; and the violence of this "meeting of the waters," about fifty feet below the frail bridge where we stood, was fearfully grand. While we were looking at it, fortunately a gleam of sunshine came out, and instantly a beautiful rainbow was formed by the spray, and hung in mid air suspended over the awful gorge.

On going into the châlet above the fall, we were informed that a bridge had broken down near Guttanen, and that it would be impossible to proceed for some time: accordingly we were kept in our drenched condition for an hour, when some travellers arrived from Meyringen, and told us that there had been a trifling accident, but that we could now cross. On arriving at the spot, I was much inclined to suspect that the whole story was a ruse to make us eat and drink the more in the Handeck Inn, for only a few planks had been carried away, and though there might perhaps have been some difficulty with mules, the gap was certainly not larger than a pedestrian might have crossed with a very slight leap. Near Guttanen the rain happily ceased, and we had time to walk ourselves tolerably dry before arriving at Reichenbach, where we enjoyed a good dinner at the Hotel des Alpes.

Here we met an old friend and his brother, and next morning walked in company with them to Rosenlaui, the *beau idéal* of Swiss scenery, where we spent the middle of the day in an excursion to the glacier. This was more beautiful than when I had seen it in former years, for in the constant progress of the ice it had changed the form of its extremity and formed a vast cavern, as blue as the sky above, and rippled like a frozen ocean. A few steps cut in the rock enabled us to walk completely under this, and feast our eyes upon one of the loveliest objects in creation. The glacier was all around divided by numberless fissures of the same exquisite colour, and the finest wood-strawberries were growing in abundance but a few yards from the ice. There is no village of Rosenlaui, but the inn stands in a charming spot, close to the bank of the stream which, lower down, forms the

Reichenbach fall, and embosomed in the richest of pinewoods, while the fine form of the Wellhorn looking down upon it completes the picture. In the afternoon we walked over the Great Scheideck to Grindelwald, stopping to pay a visit to the Upper glacier by the way; but we were again overtaken by bad weather, and arrived at the hotel in such a state that the landlord's wardrobe was in great request.

The clouds by this time seemed to have done their worst, for a lovely day succeeded, which we determined to devote to an ascent of the Faulhorn. Every tree and bush were still dripping with warm moisture, and this always proves the most fatiguing weather for mountain climbing: we arrived at the top, however, in about four hours, and being there joined by an old acquaintance, we resolved to enjoy ourselves; accordingly a messenger was despatched a few hundred feet down the mountain to fill a tub with snow, in which sundry bottles of champagne were buried, and while dinner was preparing we stretched ourselves out on the summit to admire the view. Beautiful undoubtedly it was, but I had seen it under much more remarkable circumstances in 1854. We had then left Grindelwald just as a thunderstorm was dying away, and we hoped to find good weather up above; but the rain, which had nearly ceased, began again, and we were struck by the rapidly increasing cold as we ascended. Two thirds of the way up were completed when the rain was exchanged for snow, with which the ground was thickly covered, and before we arrived at the top the snow and mist became so thick that we could not see one another at more than twenty yards distance, and it became difficult to pick our way over the rough and thickly covered ground. Shivering with cold we turned into bed with a double allowance of clothes, and slept comfortably while the wind howled round the lonely house, 8500 feet above the sea: when I awoke, the wall and the window looked equally dark, but in another hour I found I could just see the form of the latter; so I jumped out of bed, and forced it open, though with some difficulty from the frost and the quantities of snow heaped up against it. A row of huge icicles hung down from the edge of the roof, and anything more wintry than the whole prospect could not well be imagined; but the sudden appearance of the great mountains in front was so startling that I felt no inclination to move towards bed again. The snow which had collected upon the window had increased the darkness, so that when I looked out I was surprised to find that the daylight

THE WETTERHORN

was soon lost, and the … an would evidently
rise be… … … … … … … stars were
still …; the sky was cloudless overhead, though
… … mists lay thousands of feet below us in
the valleys … wreathed around the feet of the mountains, and adding to the splendour of their lofty
summits … … soon dressed and out of the
house … … … tal approach of dawn,
the … … … ast more … the
… … … … pon us … … ally
… … se obscurity of the even… … …
… … … Wetterhorn!" … some one, as its
sum… … … … … of dawn: and in
a few moments … double … the Schreckhorn
followed its example; peak after peak seemed
warmed with life, the Jungfrau b… d even more
beautifully than her neighbours, and … … the
Wetterhorn in the East to th… … bel in the
West, a long row of fire glowed …
truly worthy of th… …
severe; our …
guished from the …
to the depth of a fe…
we heartily enjoyed … …
Giessbach falls, …
At noon the day …

was considerable, and that the sun would evidently rise before long. Only the brightest of the stars were still shining; the sky was cloudless overhead, though small curling mists lay thousands of feet below us in the valleys, wreathed around the feet of the mountains, and adding to the splendour of their lofty summits. We were soon dressed and out of the house, watching the gradual approach of dawn, thoroughly absorbed in the first near view of the Oberland giants, which broke upon us unexpectedly after the intense obscurity of the evening before. "Look at the Wetterhorn!" cried some one, as its summit gleamed with the first rose of dawn: and in a few moments the double crest of the Schreckhorn followed its example; peak after peak seemed warmed with life, the Jungfrau blushed even more beautifully than her neighbours, and soon, from the Wetterhorn in the East to the Wildstrubel in the West, a long row of fires glowed upon mighty altars, truly worthy of the gods. The frost was very severe; our sleeping place could hardly be distinguished from the snow around it, which had fallen to the depth of a foot during the past evening, and we heartily enjoyed a rough scramble down to the Giesbach falls, where we soon found a warm climate. At noon the day before at Grindelwald the thermometer could not have stood at less than 100° Fahr. in the sun; and in the evening, judging from the icicles formed, and the state of the windows, there must have been at least twelve degrees of frost, thus giving a change of 80° during a few hours.

On the last occasion, however, we enjoyed the view in all the warmth of a summer's day, and returned down the mountain to Grindelwald in time for the late *table d'hôte*. In the steepest part of this descent I felt a slight wrench in my left ankle, which had been severely sprained a few months previously, and on arriving at the hotel I found myself very uncomfortably lame. Half afraid that my walking for the season was brought to an untimely end, I nevertheless took the best remedy I knew of: tying up the foot in a towel soaked in cold water, I went to sleep, and on waking in the morning found scarcely the least trace of annoyance; and by wearing for the future an elastic bandage, which I carried in case of need, I suffered no inconvenience through the remainder of our journey.

After breakfast we started, in company with our two friends, for the Wengern Alp and Interlaken. A very pleasant hour was spent at the Hôtel de la Jungfrau, as the little châlet inn calls itself, right in face of that splendid mountain, whose precipices, together with those of the Mönch and Eiger, have a sheer descent of many thousand feet into a deep gorge which receives all the masses of icy ruin that perpetually descend from the upper glaciers. This time, however, we neither saw nor heard one of these avalanches, though in 1855, when Dundas and I slept at the same inn on the Wengern Alp, we heard many a roar in the night, and early in the morning were startled out of bed by a crash like thunder; on throwing open the window we saw a cloud of snow and pulverised ice, out of which seemed to fall a cascade of water over the vast precipice, bounding from rock to rock as it descended to the bottom of the gorge. On examining this, however, with a telescope, we could see that it was a vast stream of ice, partly reduced to powder and partly preserving its huge blocks, whose course could be traced with the glass from top to bottom. One of the " toppling crags of ice" had fallen from the upper part of the mountain, and left a very perceptible blue shade on the precipitous surface which it left behind. The last echo of its ruin had scarcely died away, when the tops of the Jungfrau, Mönch, and Eiger were crimsoned with the approach of day, and seemed illuminated by the spirit of hope triumphing over the abomination of desolation.

We left the Wengern Alp sooner than we wished, for clouds were beginning to gather ominously among the mountains in the west, and before arriving at Lauterbrunnen we saw the effect of a thunderstorm in the direction of the Blumlis Alp; it soon swept across to the Jungfrau behind us, and fortunately we escaped with only a few heavy drops of rain. On approaching Lauterbrunnen we observed that the Staubbach had very little water in it, which was owing to the scarcity of snow in the winter:

> "And, like a downward smoke, the slender stream
> Along the cliff to fall and pause and fall did seem."

The rest of Tennyson's charming description from the "Lotus Eaters" applies admirably to the valley of Lauterbrunnen, and still more so to the Hasli Thal:

> "A land of streams! some, like a downward smoke,
> Slow-dropping veils of thinnest lawn, did go;
> And some through wavering lights and shadows broke,
> Rolling a slumbrous sheet of foam below."

We did not, however, linger long, but, walking briskly down the valley by the bank of the rushing Lutschine, arrived at Interlaken in about two hours;

and, having now completed what may perhaps be considered as the first act of a tour in Switzerland, we resolved to spend a day or two quietly in the great gathering-place of the *voyageurs*.

CHAP. III.

Passage of the Strahleck from the Grimsel to Grindelwald. — Crossing the Glacier. — "Das ist der Mond." — Sleep in the Hut. — A portable Wine-cellar. — Precipitous Ascent. — View from the Summit. — Descent to Grindelwald by the Lower Glacier.

In the month of August, 1855, Dundas and I had agreed to cross the celebrated pass of the Strahleck before leaving the Oberland, if weather and circumstances would permit; and accordingly we started from Grindelwald on the afternoon of the 19th, and arrived at the top of the Faulhorn, with the view of sleeping there, and going over the Scheideck to Meyringen and the Grimsel. The reason for adopting this course was that we wished to cross the Strahleck towards Grindelwald, and perhaps to pass a day or two at the Grimsel beforehand, so as to get our feet a little into ice-practice for the summer. The passage is often effected from the Grindelwald side; but the ascent must be very laborious, and the face must be turned away from the best part of the prospect, both in ascending and descending: besides, the hut over the Aar Glacier, which was used extensively by the Professors Forbes and Agassiz, being only three hours' walk from the Grimsel Hospice is a great advantage as a sleeping-place, and enables those who cross the Strahleck to cut off three dull hours from their chief day's work.

We arrived at the Hospice on a beautiful evening, and before going to bed had a conversation with the landlord, or rather with the head-waiter, who is the factotum of the establishment and a very good fellow, upon the plan for crossing the glaciers to Grindelwald; and, as his opinion was decidedly in favour of the fine weather lasting, we determined to see the guides he recommended after breakfast in the morning, and make arrangements with them for a start in the evening. While supper was preparing I was greatly amused by seeing a grand scene enacted by a guide and his master for the time being, a Scotch laird who had been confiding to me his regret at having allowed himself to be inveigled from his grouse-shooting by the entreaties of his wife and daughter. Happening to pass, I saw him violently gesticulating at the guide, who evidently was trying hard to make him understand something in an unknown tongue; he called to me and begged me to tell him what the fellow wanted, as he could not understand a word of the language: so I undertook the task of interpreter, and found that Madame was going to be carried down to Meyringen in a *chaise-à-porteur*, and that the porters, after seeing her ladyship, declared her to be "embonpoint outre mesure," and insisted on two extra pair of hands. The poor laird was so disgusted already that I could not venture to interpret this insult fully, but contented myself with fighting his battle for him: the struggle happily ended in the defeat of his adversaries, who were compelled to carry Madame with the usual number of bearers, while I received the warmest thanks of Monsieur for saving him from some danger, the nature of which he never fairly comprehended.

After breakfast next morning we were introduced to two guides named Anderegg Melchior and Johann Höckler, both of whom looked very promising fellows; and after a short conversation, we agreed to start with them for the glacier hut about four o'clock in the afternoon. Meanwhile we determined to occupy the first half of the day with a run over to the Rhone glacier, on the other side of the Grimsel pass: there we spent some time on the ice, and, after a very hot pull up the Meienwand, returned to the Hospice about three o'clock. Here we found our two guides making various preparations for the start, and bustling about with veils twisted round their

PREPARATIONS.

hats, which showed clearly enough that they had got something of an expedition in view. A good guide can turn his hand to a great many things, and Melchior soon showed a taste for cobblery by putting some right good hob-nails with rather pointed ends into the gaps made in our shoes by the last week's walking. In the next place, a young lad was engaged as porter, and sent on ahead of us towards the hut with a large basket on his back, in which blankets, provisions, and a few knives, with a very small supply of crockery, had been carefully packed for the evening's consumption and the night's comfort. At last everything was reported ready, and soon after four o'clock we sallied forth from the Hospice; our knapsacks were already on their way to Grindelwald *viâ* Meyringen on the back of a stout porter, as our guides for the pass would have quite work enough to carry the provisions in addition to the axe and ropes, and we were rather glad not to have any extra weight through what is generally considered rather a hard day's work. At starting, Melchior carried a knapsack with provisions, and fastening the good coil of rope to its straps, he walked away, using instead of an ordinary *bâton* that capital combination of axe and pole which is so well known at Chamonix. Höckler carried the cellar, which consisted of a large tin vessel with straps attached, so that it could be carried on the shoulders like a knapsack, and from its size I am afraid many people would have thought we intended to camp out for a week.

We went rather slowly over the path among the rocks which leads from the Hospice to a large and nearly desolate plain, through which the Aar finds its way from the foot of the lower glacier, until, joined by the stream from the upper glacier, it rushes on towards the Handeck fall. As we crossed this flat valley, we overtook a German gentleman who entered into conversation with our guides, the result of which was a proposition in due form, to the effect that the German's ambition being fired at the idea of our expedition, he was very desirous to accompany us. Finding that the guides had no objection to his joining the party, and that there were supplies enough for all, we consented; and he then informed us that he had only come out with the intention of a few hours' walk from the Hospice, when he had the good fortune to meet us on our way to what he was sure he should thoroughly enjoy.

We were not long in getting to the glacier; and after a very rough scramble up the moraine and the steep rocky path which leads to it, we were glad enough to find ourselves upon tolerably smooth ice, which was not much crevassed: easy, however, as the walking was, the German was continually getting behindhand, and on crossing the moraine towards our sleeping-place, we had to wait some time for him, feeling sure he could not find his way over alone. Pursuing a course nearly at right angles to the general direction of the glacier, we arrived at the foot of its rocky wall, and though we could at first see no means of getting up this, we soon found that our guides knew the way well: we followed in their steps among clefts and crannies of the rocks, the general direction of which was tolerably perpendicular for several hundred feet, and about seven in the evening, we stood at the door of the hut which was to be our hotel for the present. Just before we arrived at this point, the whole party simultaneously came to a stand-still under the influence of a strangely beautiful scene. Shut in by immense mountains, the path from the glacier was dark enough to compel us to take care of our footing, and the moon had up to this time been hidden from us by the great ridge of rocky mountains which divides the upper from the lower glacier, when suddenly, as we continued rapidly ascending, she showed herself in full splendour exactly on the summit of the ridge, bathing the long streaks of snow with a brilliancy which made them look like streams of silver, coursing down the mountain sides towards the dark depths of the glacier below. It was indeed a most exquisite sight; and all the party watched it for a few minutes in silent admiration, till the voice of the boy broke the utter stillness of the scene, and by his remark of "*Das ist der Mond*," reminded us that there is only one step from the sublime to the ridiculous. There was something so absurd in the poor fellow explaining that the moon was really the cause of the beauty before us, that both the guides and ourselves were obliged to have a hearty laugh at him. Soon after we reached the hut, the moon was once more hidden by a lofty peak, and then as we stood in the darkness, the picture became one of enchanting beauty: the long and gloomy glacier stretched out almost under our feet, and the deep shadows cast by the mountains in front of us, served as a splendid foil to the surpassing beauty of the Finsteraarhorn and its lofty snows, illuminated by the moon which was now concealed from us.

We were roused from a contemplative fit by Melchior recommending us to go into the hut; and as he held out prospects of supper and rest, both of which we knew were valuable on the mountains, we complied with his request. The hut is divided into two compartments, one of which is devoted to the guides and the other to the travellers: there is also a very small den by way of *cuisine*, and here the boy lost no time in lighting a fire, from a small stock of wood brought for the purpose from below. The travellers' room was tolerably large, and was divided into two nearly equal parts by a board about a foot wide placed on its edge: in front of this partition, a table and bench constituted the furniture of a sitting-room, while on the other side of it a thick coating of hay, with the aid of the blankets, made a very good sleeping accommodation. Cold mutton and hot *café au lait* with bread and cheese formed the main part of our supper, after which we produced the wine, and with the aid of a pipe passed the evening pleasantly enough. We rolled ourselves up in the blankets about nine o'clock, and should have slept very comfortably if human creatures had been the only inhabitants of the hay beds on which we were laid out like a row of mummies. I contrived, however, to sleep pretty well, till the sound of the door-latch woke me; and looking up, I saw Melchior's dark figure in front of me: he said it was half past three o'clock, and time to get ready for breakfast; so we jumped up, and were soon engaged in discussing more of the coffee and mutton, in company with the German, who had thus far accompanied us.

His courage, however, had by this time failed, I suppose; for with very little prelude he told us he did not think the expedition would suit him, and he should therefore take the opportunity of returning with the porter. We made no attempts to detain him, and as we with our two guides turned to the right from the hut about five o'clock, he and the lad went down to the left towards the Grimsel.

A scrambling and precipitous path, not unlike that which we had ascended the previous evening, led us down in about a quarter of an hour to the Lauteraar glacier, which we at once began to cross towards the Finsteraarhorn. The ice is perfectly easy for walking; just sufficiently crevassed to give good opportunities for a jump now and then, but not so as to present any difficulties; arriving at the moraine, we soon crossed it, and found ourselves on the Unteraar glacier, where it winds round the foot of a long spur from the Schreckhörner, or Peaks of Terror. A slight frost on the surface of the glacier was the natural consequence of a starlight night, and made the footing excellent as we kept on our way, gradually though slowly ascending; the air was delightfully fresh, and presently the sun announced his presence by a rosy light upon the upper part of the Finsteraarhorn, which, full in front of us at this moment, showed its inaccessible precipices stretching from the summit down to the very edge of the glacier, through a height of about 7000 feet. About this part of the route we found ourselves among some treacherous snow on the glacier, partially and sometimes entirely concealing the crevasses underneath; and we were therefore obliged to be cautious in probing the snow till we got upon safer footing. As we rounded the end of the long spur-like ridge that runs southward from the Schreckhörner, the effect of the increasing sunlight began to be very beautiful, and the long sharp-edged shadows on the steep snow-beds of the Finsteraarhorn were very remarkable. A fine photograph of this scene was taken by Bisson, within a day or two of our crossing the pass, and even those who were never fortunate enough to see the reality, must have been struck with the representation in the shops of London.

Once round this corner and our way for a long distance was plainly spread before us. The Finsteraarhorn and its shoulder were on our left-hand; the long spur which terminates in the double peak of the Schreckhörner was on our right; and our course lay along a huge valley of pretty smooth ice, slowly but steadily ascending between the two. About eight o'clock, we came to a large stone quite unconsciously performing its destined journey down the glacier; and resolving to treat this as a table in the wilderness, we prepared at once for that second breakfast which is so particularly agreeable on the mountains. The sun being by this time pretty warm, we began by putting the wine-cellar down on the ice, and heaping snow over it, so that when we had finished the rest of our meal we found the liquor in capital order, and fit for a prince. We soon set out again, and the further we ascended the glacier, the more we found it covered with fresh snow, into which we sank considerably. About this time, too, we began to wonder where the pass could be; to all appearances we were taking a great deal of trouble to enter a complete *cul de sac*. On each side of us was an inaccessible chain, as I have described, and these, meeting at the further end of this glacier valley, seemed to shut us off from all hopes of getting to the Grindelwald side of the vast obstruction; we knew, however, that the pass was there, and presently the guides pointed out the place where we were to scale the seeming perpendicular walls of this rocky fortress. Full in front of us there was a long streak of snow lying at an amazingly steep angle, and bounded on both sides by the most unpromising of rocks; this was the Strahleck, the "sunbeam corner," as its name implies, and as we approached nearer we felt the full force of the appellation. The snow became softer every minute that we advanced, for the slope increased rapidly, and the heat was intensely increased by the fact that the full force of the sun was shining on a surface so inclined towards it. At last the rope was produced and we advanced in line, well tied together, to the edge of the *Bergschrund,* or huge crevasse that always marks the point where the upper part of a glacier leaves the slopes from which it takes its rise and derives part of its nourishment.

Very cautiously we approached this difficulty, which in some respects answered to the moat surrounding a fortified place; the snow was so soft that we all for a few moments floundered up to the middle; but by a little perseverance we worked it down, with feet and knees, till we got a tolerably firm footing at the narrowest part of the crevasse that we could find. The snow slope in front of us here projected a little, so that with the support of the rope from behind, Melchior at once leant forward and began to make a few large holes in it, using his fists to batten them down and make them as firm as possible. The heat and glare were now terrific: in spite of veils, the skin felt almost scorching, and the steep-lying snow, over which we had to ascend, was so completely dripping in this natural furnace that we could not help thinking that the principal danger consisted in the probability of the whole mass coming down with a run, as soon as the first man trusted his weight to it. However, Melchior, seeming satisfied with the good lodgment he had provided for his feet, made a sign of caution and steadiness to the rest of the party, and then threw himself forward upon the wall of snow, getting his feet into the lower, and his right hand into the upper, of the holes he had made, keeping his axe still in the left hand. It was an exciting moment; but he kept his footing safely, and finding the snow did not give way, he moved two or three steps further up through the snow which rose above his knees; then he turned round to us, and after treading down a good landing-place, he beckoned to me to advance; directly I did so, however, the snow on our side of the crevasse gave way, and I went through up to my chest. Melchior had a firm hold of the rope, and pounding down the snow with my knees I soon made a better footing, and then following his steps over the crevasse, with the aid of a twitch from the rope, soon stood by his side. Dundas followed in the same way, and then Höckler with the wine-cellar. It was a great satisfaction to find the snow bear us all together, and we felt the more confidence as we continued the ascent in single file. In about ten minutes we came to a place where some rocks encroached upon the snow, and as they seemed rough enough for good walking, in spite of their steepness, we floundered out of the snow towards the right, and had a few moments' halt on *terra firma*. Up to this time Melchior had not spoken a word since crossing the *Bergschrund*, and we of course followed his example; here, however, the most dangerous part was over, and we enjoyed a good scramble up the rocks for a few minutes, when we were again obliged to take to the snow; continuing the same line of ascent, and in much the same fashion as before, we arrived at the summit of the Strahleck and landed safely on its rocky crest. Owing to the softness of the snow, we had climbed in little more than twenty minutes what sometimes takes more than two hours, when the hardness of the ice requires steps to cut through the whole distance; I cannot help thinking though, that, from the state of the snow, the danger was greater than in the slower method of ascent. The height of this steep part is, I believe, about 500 feet, and amazingly near the perpendicular, so there was no small risk of the snow coming down in a body on being disturbed at the bottom, and burying us in the crevasse.

Arrived at the summit we set to work to enjoy the prospect thoroughly, while Höckler buried the wine-flask in the snow, and Melchior prepared to set on bread and mutton for dinner. Sitting with our faces to the south, we had the splendid peaks of the Schreckhörner close on our left, now not much higher than ourselves, and looking very much as if the ascent could be made, with some difficulty, from near where we were: straight away from beneath our feet the long line of the Aar glacier, radiant with the fresh snow over which we had travelled, extended itself till terminated by the peaks which divide it from the Oberaar glacier, while to the right arose the vast precipices of the Finsteraarhorn, the summit of which was seen to the greatest perfection, presenting, however, a very different picture to the snowy obelisk which is seen from the Faulhorn. A little further round to the right the huge side of the Eiger terminating in a knife-like edge, and part of the back of the Mönch and Jungfrau seemed close beside us, completing a glorious panorama of the high summits in the very centre of which we were stationed. Turning round towards to north, bed after bed of pure snow, alternating with rocks, led steeply down towards the lower glacier of Grindelwald, marking the general course of our descent to the valley, which, with its lovely verdure, afforded a striking contrast to the desolate and tremendous grandeur immediately round us. On the other side of the valley, and right over the range of which the Wengern Alp and Faulhorn form a part, the lake of Thun shone like a beautiful mirror among its hills, with the Niesen and Stockborn conspicuous at its further extremity; and still further the eye wandered over the vast plain country to the north-west, and, dwelling for a moment upon the distant sheet of the lake of Neuchâtel, lost itself in the blue mountains near the French frontier.

Such was the magnificent view presented to us, seated quietly upon the narrow neck of this wonderful ridge, the summit of our ambition for the present. It was about ten o'clock; not a cloud marred the face of the heavens, and not a sound broke the solemn silence that reigned about us, except the occasional fall of avalanches at the back of the Mönch or Eiger, while the air was so perfectly still that a lucifer was not blown out, even in this exposed situation. A beautiful butterfly, with most aspiring courage, tempted by the brilliancy of the upper world far above his usual haunts, fluttered over the ridge close by us, and started off joyously towards the old Hospice of the Grimsel.

Meanwhile the wine had been deliciously iced, and, after the broiling which we had endured, formed an excellent termination to our early dinner. We then began to descend rapidly over long ledges of snow, varied with occasional scrambles down the rocks, and had some capital *glissades*, sitting down one behind the other as close as we could, and each holding the legs of the man behind him, while our alpenstocks lay across our laps. One of these slides was a particularly long one, and over lumpy uneven snow, the effect of which was that the severe jolting broke our train in the middle, and, shouting with laughter, we raced down the remainder of it in two divisions, without sustaining any injury but the loss of a brandy-flask. Some more rocks succeeded, and then we had to cross obliquely over a wide incline of hard snow, almost in the state of ice; we were not, however, tied together, and after getting over a great part of it, I took a careless step and lost my footing. In a moment I was flying down like a flash of lightning: in vain I tried to stop myself by leaning on the point of my alpenstock, for the ice was hard; I did not, however, lose my presence of mind, and succeeded in steering myself a little, but on looking down I saw a sea of crevasses towards which I was helplessly flying, and the prospect was getting very serious, when luckily I shot into a small crevasse large enough to stop me and not large enough to injure me; so I soon extricated myself and climbed cautiously enough towards where Melchior was descending to meet me in an agony of fear for my safety. After getting down some steep and difficult rocks, where we were let down, one by one, to various narrow ledges with the help of the rope, we at last arrived upon the upper part of the Grindelwald glacier, and in time found ourselves once more on firm land at the top of the narrow path winding down to the valley, along the side of the glacier which it sometimes almost overhangs. At about half-past four o'clock we were once more in the Aigle Hotel, where we found the porter waiting with the knapsacks which he had brought round from the Grimsel. We had both enjoyed most fully the passage of the Strahleck, and there are few expeditions of equal importance which can be made at so little expense. The guides asked thirty francs each and a *bonnemain*, which, considering the long march they would have to return, was not at all too much; in addition to this, the porter to the hut had six francs, and we considered that, in the delight of the day's adventures, we were very fully repaid for all cost and trouble. The whole journey from the Hospice might be easily performed in a long day, but it is undoubtedly far preferable to sleep at the hut; as, in addition to the fact of three dull hours being cut off from the beginning of the main day's work, there is the inestimable advantage of arriving at the pass itself two hours before noon, when, on a hot day, the scorching would be almost intolerable.

CHAP. IV.

Interlaken.— Kandersteg.— The Œschinen See.— Schwarenbach. — An old Friend. — Ascent of the Great Altels. — Singular Glacier. — Adventure on the Summit. — Cloudy Weather. — The Gemmi. — Leukerbad. — The Ladders.

THERE is a good deal of truth in Albert Smith's description of Interlaken, as a street full of lodging-houses. The crowds of people of all sorts and nations who resort to it during the season, with the crowds of carriages starting for and coming back from the various excursions in the neighbourhood, make it too little of a change from the busy life endured by most of us throughout the greater part of the year. Its situation, too, is low and completely shut in by mountains, so that the atmosphere is somewhat enervating, and the heat very excessive. Yet, after all, it is a pleasant place for a short stay; everybody meets acquaintances there, and the verandahs of the hotels, with their rows of oleanders and bright flowers, make very agreeable places for a chat in the summer evenings. Besides the excursions on the lakes of Thun and Brienz, there are plenty of drives for those who do not like walking at all, and still more short excursions for indifferent pedestrians; so that it must always be a popular place of resort. The beautiful view of the fair Jungfrau, filling up the distance between the green mountains on each side of the valley of Lanterbrunnen, is also a great attraction; and even those who do not like the trouble of penetrating nearer to the snowy mountains can every day enjoy seeing one of the finest of them at a distance.

Those, however, who derive the highest gratification from the bracing air and active life which is only to be found in the wilder parts of the country, are generally glad to shake off the dust of Interlaken from their feet; and I must confess that, after spending a day on the lake of Thun, and another in a climb through the woods up to the Crétin hospital, from which there is a really very delightful view of the lake of Brienz and the surrounding country, I was by no means sorry to find the carriage at the door on the morning of the third day to take us to Kandersteg, on our way to the Gemmi.

The upper parts of the mountains had been powdered with fresh snow in the night, and, as this is always considered a sign of good weather coming, we looked forward with great satisfaction to the prospect of our next week's campaign.

The road is carried along the banks of the lake of Thun as far as the village of Spiez, soon after which it turns sharply round to the left, and skirts the base of the Niesen, after passing the end of the Simmenthal, the view of which is quite enough to tempt one strongly towards its beauties. For several miles the Kienthal was now in front of us, with the triple-crowned Blumlis Alp at the head of it, presenting the same aspect as when seen from Berne, only, of course, on a much larger scale. A guide once told me a curious legend about the Blumlis Alp, and, though I do not remember all the details, I know the leading fact of it was, that the mountain was formerly covered with luxurious pasture, till it was suddenly changed into a snowy waste, to punish a peasant for some offence against the world of spirits.

We had an early dinner at Frutigen while the horse rested, and, as our driver seemed to be an unreasonably long time about his own refreshment, we sent for him, but were informed that he was drinking schnaps at a great rate in the inn, and was not ready; so we ordered him out immediately; but very soon after starting it became pretty clear that he was not altogether sober, and somewhat disposed to impertinence. At a few miles beyond Frutigen we all got out to walk up a long hill, and he took the opportunity of getting into a quarrel with some lads by the road-side; hoping he would get a good thrashing, we left him, and led the horse on to the top of the hill, where he was put into a trot and the *cocher* entirely abandoned; but he caught us on the next hill, which was very long and steep, thoroughly blown, but evidently somewhat steadied. We were now in the Kander valley, with the fine snowy mass of the Great Altels in front, and were not much longer in arriving at Kandersteg itself.

Here I must say something about the accommodation to be found at Kandersteg. Some travellers have abused it not a little, and certain remarks to be seen in the Livres des Étrangers at other places would lead anyone to believe it a den of thieves. Mr. Wills says it is "a halting-place which all who value a good night's rest should religiously eschew;" adding, however, that in 1854 he saw symptoms of what was apparently intended for a new hotel; about which, if opened, he did not wish to express an opinion. When I was first there in 1854 the inn had certainly acquired rather an unenviable notoriety in various ways, under the auspices of a somewhat disreputable old lady who had kept it for some time, but was then, as I was informed, under notice to quit. On arriving at Leukerbad the next day, I found from the head waiter of the Hôtel des Alpes that he had made the necessary arrangements for opening the inn at Kandersteg in time for the next season; and, accordingly, in the last two years I have found him established in the old house, which he has thoroughly set to rights, and re-christened by the name of the Hotel Victoria. He speaks English better than most foreigners, and takes every pains to make himself and his house agreeable to visitors. The aforesaid old lady has vowed revenge, and, though not heard of in 1855, she employed her time most probably in preparing the sinews of war, for last season a new house was hastily built by her, and called the Hôtel de l'Ours. It is only a châlet inn, but, being placed very near the foot of the Gemmi, no doubt many people in their way northward were inveigled into it by the guides, who are regularly paid by the proprietors of new houses to bring travellers under their hospitable roofs. I believe the higher class of guides to be above such trickery; but it is certain that many of the men whom one finds about the Oberland will recommend a new hotel if there is one in the place, even though the walls are but half dry, for the sake of the half franc which they receive from the landlord. Possibly the old lady of the Ours may repent of her ways in the new house; but, knowing her antecedents, I think it only fair to the landlord of the Victoria to say that it was he who undertook to whitewash the reputation of Kandersteg, and that he has already succeeded in changing its ancient state of dirt into one of cleanliness and comfort.

After dismissing our little coachman with a lecture upon the disadvantages of drunkenness, we set out towards the beautiful little Œschinen See, and arrived at its edge in rather more than an hour. Mr. Wills's description of this lovely lake does not do it more than justice; and it is to be regretted that so many persons cross the Gemmi without devoting a few hours to visiting one of the most remarkable spots in the whole country. It is the only lake I have ever seen which washes the actual base of a vast precipitous mountain like the Blumlis Alp, whose pure snowy form is completely reflected upon its surface, only rippled on the further side by the dash of streams, as they leap from the huge sides of the mountain right down into the mirror beneath them. When I saw it in August, 1855, the effect was heightened by a thunderstorm in the evening: the dense cloud caused such darkness, that it was very difficult to keep our footing; but every now and then, as a flash of lightning flew through the obscurity, the awful form of the Blumlis Alp was revealed for a moment:

> "Vast images of glimmering dawn
> Are half discovered, and withdrawn."

This year, however, we did not see the lake to any great advantage, as the evening was neither perfectly fine nor yet perfectly stormy; dull clouds hung about the scene, sometimes veiling a considerable part of it: we returned, therefore, towards Kandersteg, falling in on our way with a peasant who lived in a châlet not far above the village. I spoke to this man about the mountains in general, and the Altels in particular; whereupon he declared that he had been on the summit a short time ago with a Herr and another man, and that it might be ascended in seven hours from the Schwarenbach. My fancy was rather fired by the idea of making this ascent, and I took down the man's name with a view to future inquiries, but without any serious intentions in that direction at present. It was nearly dark when we returned to our inn, and the landlord had just got our supper all ready; after which he had a long chat with us, and let us into the secret of several little mysteries connected with the guide and porter system. Among other good arrangements at this much-abused place, he has a kind of staff of his own in the village, ready to act as guides or porters at a fixed charge, which may be paid beforehand to the master by way of preventing any disputes afterwards.

In the morning he produced one of these domestics, who was to carry two knapsacks to the top of the Gemmi Pass for four francs, which was certainly not a heavy charge. We started soon after breakfast, and passing by mine hostess of the Ours, we began the climb through a forest of pines, with quantities of ferns and flowers growing about their roots. At length the steep ascent came to an end, and we found ourselves on a wild plateau of high land with the Altels forming a magnificent pyramid of ice upon our left, and the Rinderhorn, apparently not much lower, a little beyond it on the same side. The magnificently white and unbroken glacier which covers the side of the Altels had often attracted my admiration before; and now, with the evening's conversation fresh in my mind, I could not help observing it with increased interest. Mr. Wills says that he and Balmat looked at it with longing eyes, and thought it might be practicable for an ascent. I thought so too, and was rather full of my subject, when we arrived at the little Schwarenbach inn, the only habitation between Kandersteg and Leukerbad. It has been very prudently built in a sort of natural amphitheatre, the rocks behind protecting it in a semicircle from the northern blasts, while those in front rise like a lofty wall, only open at the point where the road winds away to the Gemmi. Intending to have luncheon here, we walked into the little *salle à manger*, where I found a party of foreigners inspecting one of the closets filled with chamois and châlets cut out of wood, which are so common in Switzerland, while the manufacturer of them with his apron of green baize was showing them off for sale. At first I noticed the profile only of this man, but thought I knew something about it; in another moment he happened to turn his full face towards me, and whom should I see, in the person of this carver of graven images, but our old guide over the Strahleck, Anderegg Melchior? I greatly disconcerted and surprised his customers, by rushing at him with a How d'ye do? in German, and a hearty shake of the hand, which he returned with interest. We were really delighted to see one another again; but after exchanging a few words I told him to proceed with his business, and talk to me afterwards. While we discussed some bread and cheese, I fancy he disposed of some of his carvings; and when the other people were gone he came up to us again. It appeared that he had settled in the Schwarenbach, as he had a good offer of being carver in ordinary to the inn: surrounded also by a splendid mountain country, with which he was well acquainted, he was always ready to act as guide to those who might require his services in that capacity. I told him of my having fallen in with the man who said he had ascended the Altels; but, upon my mentioning his name, Melchior at once said that he knew all about that expedition; he had seen them start and fail in their attempt after some hours, finding the ice too steep for them. He however brought out his own book of certificates, one of which stated that he had lately made the ascent himself with two Englishmen; he confirmed the other man's opinion that about seven hours would be the time of ascending, and three or four for the descent. He said, too, that knowing from experience I could take pretty good care of myself, he should be quite ready to go alone with me; so in five minutes we arranged to start on the next morning. Both my brother and B. proved very good walkers, but not being so enthusiastic as myself about mountain-climbing, they agreed to go on to Leukerbad, while I remained to sleep at Schwarenbach.

I wished however to introduce them to the first grand view from the top of the Gemmi, and leaving my knapsack at the house, I walked on with them at one o'clock. We were soon on the dreary mule-path which runs along the side of the Daubensee, the dreariness of the scene around being only broken by the splendid appearance of the Lämmern glacier and the snowy masses of the Wildstrubel on our right. Presently leaving the path, we ran up a rough slope of grass and mountain flowers, and then a single step, like the wand of a magician, changed the kingdom of desolation into a scene of marvellous beauty. All was perfectly clear and bright before us. Two thousand feet below was Leukerbad, of which we could see little beyond the roofs of the houses, and the winding Dala flowed shining down its valley, shut in on both sides with magnificent cliffs from every cleft of which rose the dark pine-trees, looking smaller and smaller till lost in the great valley of the Rhone, beyond which shone in the bright blue sky, at distances of from thirty to forty miles, the vast peaks of the Monte Rosa country. I felt an indescribable pleasure at again recognising the Weisshorn, the Matterhorn, and the Dent Blanche, looking like a party of dear old friends; and after my delighted companions had gone down the pass to Leukerbad, I lingered for nearly an hour in intense enjoyment of the scene. At last I turned and walked back to the Schwarenbach.

There was no one else in the house, so I dined alone, and went out to the bench in front to have a pipe with Melchior, and talk over the prospects of the next day. As the stars came peeping out one by one, I went in for a cup of coffee, upon which the landlord entered into conversation with me. I do not know if this man is the same who was described in 1854 as a " véritable voleur," but at all events, he treated me very well, and " let's speak of a man as we find him." He appeared to me a simple sort of creature, and could not even read, as I discovered in rather a ludicrous manner: wishing, I suppose, to entertain me, he brought down from a shelf a bundle of maps with a few guide-books, prefacing their introduction to the table by saying that travellers had so often complained of his want of a library that he had felt it necessary to commence one. He then opened a small map, which he assured me was "une belle carte de la Suisse," but upon looking at it I found it was only a map on rather a large scale of the country immediately round the Gemmi. I had some difficulty in convincing him of this fact, and only succeeded by showing him Kandersteg near the top and Leukerbad not far from the bottom of it, upon which he explained that he could not read the names, and looked sadly disappointed. He soon rallied, however, and opened another, saying with some confidence, "Mais, monsieur, voilà donc une belle carte du pays!" This proved unfortunately to be the map of European railways which had been extracted from a Bradshaw! I could not help laughing as I explained this to him; and, when I asked him what he had paid for it, he replied, lifting up his hands, "Ah! monsieur, j'ai payé un franc cinquante, on m'a donc affreusement volé!" This was certainly true, as its legitimate value might be about twopence; and if he is indeed a *voleur*, it is satisfactory to know that some one had played a successful game of diamond cut diamond; but as I was disposed to take a charitable view of him, I felt really sorry that he should have been so grossly cheated. Soon after this little episode I went to bed, having arranged with Melchior to be called at half-past three, and start at half-past four o'clock in the morning.

I was aroused from a good sleep by the entrance of Melchior with a candle, and in half an hour was at breakfast, while he was engaged in hammering a few good nails into my shoes. And here I may observe that, though many people recommend the use of screws, and some condescend even to *crampons*, I have always found a good double row of hobnails round the sole and heel, with a few miscellaneous ones in the middle, quite enough for all purposes, and have never tried anything else. They ought not to be close together under the ball of the foot, except at the edges, for fear of not giving good foothold upon the rocks, and if the heads are a little pointed, so much the better.

At half-past four we walked out of the house, Melchior carrying a knapsack containing bread and cold meat with a couple of bottles of wine, to which he fastened a small coil of rope; he had also a short-handled ice-axe in his leathern belt. The stars were shining brightly, but a few white clouds in the direction of the Wildstrubel looked rather unsatisfactory; the wind however was from the north, and we had great hopes of a clearance after sunrise. Meanwhile the Altels and Rinderhorn were entirely free from even the slightest mist, so we saw our work well before us: there was the white peak which we were resolved to reach, unless the weather became so desperately bad as to compel our return.

For about twenty minutes we followed the path towards Kandersteg, and then turned off to the right, scrambling as well as we could among a wild desert of loose stones and rocks, and making a straight course for the top of the mountain. Presently we crossed a noisy little stream, and found ourselves at the base of the Great Altels, which rises at a very steep inclination from this point to its summit. For about half an hour more we ascended over grass, varied with shrubs and considerably sprinkled with large stones, and then found ourselves scrambling up loose shaly rubbish, which gave way at every step, and was so greatly inclined, that we were obliged to take a twisting course to ascend it. This was by no means improved a little higher up, when we came upon the fresh snow which had fallen two nights before, and filled up the interstices between the stones, so that some caution was necessary in selecting places to set our feet upon without running the risk of ankle-spraining. It was getting uncommonly cold too, and a sharp frost in the night had made the stones very slippery by freezing all that the last day's sun had melted of the fresh snow.

Our course lay close to the right of a kind of wide

and rocky gorge, at the top of which the icy covering of the mountain terminates abruptly in a perpendicular edge, probably not much less than 200 feet high. The vertical surface of this is rent in every direction, and marked with large fissures in the blue ice at the points where from time to time masses of it are detached from the main glacier and dashed down to the bottom of the gorge. We arrived at the edge of this tremendous parapet, and waited a few minutes to examine it from a perfectly safe place at the side, which, however, was so close that we could have pitched a stone into one of the icy caverns. It is impossible to conceive anything more completely realising Virgil's words,

> "jam, jam lapsura cadentique
> Imminet assimilis."

But, threatening and awfully dangerous as it looks, I was informed by Melchior that it descends bodily only once in about a hundred years. The inclination of the rocky bed on which it reposes is too great to admit of the glacier descending by degrees into the warmer temperature, where gradual melting would compensate for the accumulations above; consequently, its extremity increases with every winter's snow, until the vast weight can no longer be supported and falls crashing down to the valley. It is fortunate that such an event only happens once in a century, for the effect must be like an earthquake for miles around the scene of devastation caused by it. Its last fall seems to have taken place about sixty years ago. I had often admired this splendid glacier from below, but I can now say, after a close inspection of it, that it would be well worth anyone's while to ascend the mountain far enough to examine it, even if he were to return without climbing any further.

By this time the clouds showed manifest indications of increasing rather than dispersing; but time was now an object with me, and we resolved to proceed, come what might. We had previously put on our gaiters, and as the mountain was here rather deeply covered with fresh snow, they proved very useful: we mounted a long way through this, tied together at a distance of about three yards, and then finding the snowy covering thinner every moment, we stopped a short time to prepare for another style of work, and look about us a little. The effect of the now heavy clouds booming over the lesser mountains below us was very grand and singular. As their dark forms advanced, they threw shadows upon the hills far blacker than I should have thought possible; and while one was thus enveloped in obscurity, the next was in full light and beauty, rejoicing in the morning sun as it shone through a gap in the clouds. The Rinderhorn was partly veiled, which added to the grandeur of its summit, soaring over the cloud which rolled between us; but there was a perfectly clear view of the Torrenthorn a few miles to the south, and many of the peaks rising out of the Lötschen Thal. The upper part of the Altels, which we had still to surmount, shut out the view towards the Blumlis Alp and Tschingel glacier, but the view was generally very fine towards the south, where in the distance we saw many of the Monte Rosa fraternity. I always carried a small folding-up telescope by Ross, which is certainly the most convenient instrument of the kind I have seen: these glasses possess, in their lightness and small compass, a great advantage over the heavy double opera-glasses, and have far greater power for clearly distinguishing objects at long distances. When opened they are about two feet long, and shut up into a space of six inches; they only cost 2*l*. 15*s*., but I and various guides have always found, on comparing them with others, that is impossible to excel them without great power and consequent bulk. As a proof of the great steepness of the side of the

Altels, I may mention that in, taking off the little cap of this glass, I let it fall upon the snow which was quite soft on the surface, and, thinking that as its weight was so small it could not go far, I made no particular effort to save it; but away it went in a moment, and, rolling down the unbroken slope with an amazing velocity, was out of sight in a few seconds, and must soon after have been precipitated over the parapet of ice which I have just described. Watching its rapid descent, I could not help remarking to Melchior what a fate it would be for a man if he fairly lost his footing here: he, however, with his short axe in his hand, showed me how, by a powerful stroke with it, he could probably stop himself when all other hope failed, as he had secured it to his wrist by a strap, which would prevent him parting company with it easily.

We then continued our ascent, and, finding the ice hard and close to the surface, he had to cut steps for a long time; we both, however, had excellent wind, and went straight up, seldom turning a yard to the right or to the left, I always keeping exactly two steps behind him, and making it a point of honour never to let the rope tighten, which was tied round my waist and his. On looking at my watch, he was quite astonished to find what progress we had made, calling out repeatedly, "Gut, gut!" and evincing every possible sign of high satisfaction as he pointed down the long line of our track, and remarked that there were no zigzags. The weather, however, was not getting on so well as ourselves; and presently a thick cloud, preceded by a cold blast of wind, came driving down upon us and peppering us with snow. There was no time to be lost, that was clear; so, being resolved to get to the top, we pushed upwards with as much speed as a cautious regard to our footing would admit of: in this we were favoured by finding the snow soft enough for a while to enable us to dispense with the axe. The cone in front of us was rapidly becoming narrower as we approached the goal; we cared nothing now for the cold while a few more steps were being cut up a small part even steeper than the rest, and then, with a shout, we jumped together on the highest point of the Great Altels.

On looking at my watch, the time was only a quarter past eight; we had reached a summit twelve thousand feet high in three hours and three quarters. The Schwarenbach is about six thousand feet; but we had descended a considerable distance from that point before beginning the ascent of the mountain. The summit is a small rounded cone, with deep snow upon it, wreathing towards the eastern side over precipices of which we could form no idea, as we dared not go nearer to them. A thin pole about ten feet high, with an iron cross on the top, had been previously planted here by Melchior himself, as I understood; and, as we were both in the highest spirits, he climbed up this in a moment, and then shouted forth the Oberland war-whoop as if he thought anyone could possibly hear him. When he came down, I followed his example; but, unfortunately, I had forgotten to fasten the strap of my wide-awake, and a gust of wind and snow carried it off over the precipices towards the Gasteren Thal. We were still tied together for fear of accidents upon the narrow crest, so that, when Melchior made an effort to save it, he was soon brought up by his tether, though it passed within a foot of his hand. When I came down he unfastened my end of the rope, and, tying it to the post, wanted to go to the edge of the snow to see if the hat had happened to lodge close by; but the place looked too fearful, and I insisted on pulling him back. He then wanted to lend me his own; but I would not listen to such a proposal, and, tying up my head in a handkerchief, I sat down with him at the foot of the post, and could not help having a hearty laugh at the misadventure. As the cold was now rather severe, we dug holes in the snow, and buried our legs up to the knees in it; then we opened the knapsack, and prepared to enjoy our feast. Melchior is a famous chamois-hunter, and he told me that often, when benighted on the mountains, he has dug a deep hole in the snow, and slept comfortably in it till morning.

The wind was so high that the squalls passed quickly, and in the intervals between them we had many peeps of the magnificent scenery round us; and I was convinced that in fine weather the panorama from this mountain could scarcely be surpassed by any. The summit commands the whole of the Oberland group, as well as the Monte Rosa country and the Saasgrat, while to the north there is an exquisite view down the Kanderthal to the foot of the lake of Thun. All this we only saw by degrees; but it is no subject of regret to be sometimes at a great height in cloudy weather, as the alternate covering and unveiling of the scenery produces an effect little short of magical.

After staying about twenty minutes on the top we found ourselves quite cold enough to warrant a descent, so we packed up the rest of our provisions and got into harness immediately. Some of the descent over the hardest part of the ice was rather awkward work, and required the greatest caution in consequence of the excessive steepness. At such times Melchior went first, stepping in the holes he had cut in ascending, and I followed so close that my foot entered every step as his left it. When we found the snow soft enough, we took a firm hold of each other's hand, and went down side by side, taking care to keep step, and jumping firmly on our heels, but never allowing ourselves to get into anything like a run. Descending steep inclines is always much more difficult than the ascent; but in this way we moved downwards very fast, Melchior from time to time giving vent to his favourite cry of "Good, good!"

At last we got clear of the ice and snow, and found ourselves once more on the loose shale: this is capital stuff for descending over, and we went jumping down it at a great pace. By the time we reached the upper grass, rain was falling instead of snow, which made a good excuse for increased speed, particularly as my head was only tied up in a handkerchief, from the corners of which a mixture of snow and water was continually dripping; and, though the exercise kept me perfectly warm and comfortable, we made the best of our way back to the inn, arriving there at exactly eleven o'clock, only six hours and a half from the time we left it.

The astonishment of the people at the house was great, as we had completed the whole journey before they thought we could have even reached the summit: the state of the weather had prevented them from watching us, so they knew nothing of how we were getting on till our sudden appearance in person. The great peculiarity of this mountain is that its side presents one continuous slope through the whole distance, the average inclination being, I imagine, very nearly, if not quite, 45°, though I confess I had no means of accurately measuring it. The variations are very slight indeed, and we did not meet with a single crevasse to turn us out of our straight course. Under these circumstances, if the wind and legs are strong enough to enable one to dispense with long zigzags, an ascent may be made with great rapidity; and that such is the nature of the mountain may be pretty clearly understood by anyone who examines it from below with a telescope: from the summit to the tremendous wall at the foot of the glacier, the sun shines on one unbroken slope of ice and snow, glistening in its rays like a pyramid of polished silver.

I was exceedingly delighted with the success of

the ascent, which was accomplished without, I believe, a single false step. Upon consideration, however, I am inclined to doubt the prudence of two men alone going upon such an expedition. As a general rule, I am decidedly of opinion that if the travellers are more than one, each of them being really a good walker and well accustomed to the mountains, one guide apiece is quite sufficient for any expedition; but I am disposed to agree with those who think that, for excursions in the high snowy regions, the party should not consist of less than three in all,— either a single traveller and two guides, or *vice versâ*, if the two travellers have good ground for perfect confidence in themselves and in one another. On the present occasion, for instance, everything fortunately went right; but if either of us had met with any disaster, such as a sprain, a bad fall, or a sudden attack of illness,—all of which are within the bounds of possibility,—the other would have had a very difficult and dangerous task in managing the descent for both: whereas, if the party consists of three, the chances are always two to one in favour of an individual misfortune being easily got over.

After drying my hair and enjoying a pipe with a cup of coffee, I began to think of going over to Leukerbad. Melchior offered me his hat, and borrowing another for himself, insisted on going with me, in spite of the rain, which was now falling fast: remonstrance was useless; go he would, and invented a good-natured excuse about wishing to see his brother. Accordingly I paid my bill, with which I thought I had no reason to complain, and we started off arm in arm so as to divide the shelter of an umbrella between us. The squalls drove furiously across the path by the side of the Daubensee, but we had enjoyed our morning so completely, that we now felt quite above being disturbed by trifles: on reaching the summit of the pass, the rain ceased, and we were sheltered from the wind by the lofty rocks on the right; there was, however, no trace of the glorious view which we had enjoyed the day before from the same place, so without stopping a moment we hastened down the wonderful twists of the Gemmi, and arrived at the Hôtel des Alpes in Leukerbad about two o'clock in the afternoon.

Here I found my companions, and, after a short talk about the Altels, I adjourned to improve my toilet, which had been sadly disarranged by the driving rain, followed by a large deposit of mud from the Gemmi. With great regret I parted with Melchior, considering him a most excellent and trustworthy fellow, one of those true and stout hearts

with whom it is always a pleasure to be associated;
it was arranged, however, that we would, if possible,
meet again another year, and hunt the Wildstrubel
and its glaciers, with which he is well acquainted.

As soon as I was tolerably fit to be seen, and
equipped with a reserve wide-awake of my brother's,
we made up a party of half a dozen, whom I offered
to escort to the Ladders, about half an hour's walk
from the hotel. We went off at once, and in due
time arrived by a good path through the fir woods at
this very remarkable communication between Leukerbad and the hill-village of Albinen, the inhabitants of which last only reach the rest of the world
by going up and down a system of broad ladders,
like those which are generally represented in old
pictures of Jacob's dream. We climbed up the first,
and then a few steps in the rock led to the second,
and so on for six or seven more, some of the upper
ladders standing on narrow ledges not wider than
themselves, on the face of cliffs extending several
hundred feet down to the valley beneath. We returned to the hotel in time for the evening *table-
d'hôte*, and wound up the day in a very agreeable
manner.

CHAP. V.

The Baths of Leuk. — Visp. — Effects of the Earthquake. — St. Nicolaus. — A Race. — Zermatt. — The Schwartzen See. — The Hörnli. — Magnificent View. — The Theodule and Gorner Glaciers. — Hôtel du Riffel. — Preparations for Monte Rosa.

THE first occupation in the morning at Leukerbad is to go into the bath-room, and either undergo the operation of a few hours' steaming, or content one's self by watching the effect of it upon others. We preferred the latter course, and were sufficiently amused by observing the human contents of the four large tanks, disporting themselves like "porpoises at play." About fifteen or twenty men and women, all in long blue bathing-dresses, were sitting in each of these, up to their necks in warm water, and many of them were condemned to sit there for eight hours in the day. The "sedet æternumque sedebit" of the "infelix Theseus" could hardly have been a more miserable fate; most of the occupants were of course suffering from various complaints, and the wash-house feeling of the atmosphere was most unpleasant. However, they seemed for the most part very contented with their lot; some of the ladies amused themselves with arranging bouquets, while others worked: many of the gentlemen had coffee served on little floating tables, and the greatest fun seemed to consist in making such a storm of splashing round a breakfast-eater as to compel him to bestir himself in revenge, and thereby upset his table. One tank especially was the scene of a most extensive and severe splashing-fight, in which the combatants used their trays with both hands, and dashed volumes of water over one another, amidst uproarious shouting, all which was endured with perfect calmness and good humour by a couple of Frenchwomen in a corner of the bath.

I should much have liked to spend the day in a visit to the summit of the Torrenthorn, particularly as I had made the attempt in 1854, when I was first at Leukerbad; but I had then been so severely lamed in jumping over a gate at Kandersteg, that I was obliged to let my companions go on without me for the last half of the ascent, while I returned ignominiously to the hotel. However, I had climbed high enough to get my first view of Mont Blanc, which is seen on emerging from the woods upon the first high pastures. My friends were highly delighted with the prospect from the top, which must evidently be very fine, embracing as it does the Bernese Oberland, the Monte Rosa country, the valley of the Rhone, and Mont Blanc. We were now, however, eager to get to Zermatt, and, as the weather was still unsettled, we made up our minds to go at once to Visp.

After breakfast we walked down the valley of the Dala to the miserable though picturesque town of Leuk, enjoying a fine view of the Rhone valley from the heights above it. Happening here to find an empty car, we engaged it to take us as far as Visp, where we arrived early in the evening, after stopping some time at Turtmann.

The Hôtel du Soleil had somewhat recovered from the sad state of havoc caused by the earthquake of July, 1855, and the landlord had consequently returned to his normal state of good humour. A month after the earthquake I found the house shaken from top to bottom, every wall split, mortar and stones brought tumbling to the floors, most of the rooms quite uninhabitable, and the proprietor himself looking like Marius among the ruins of Carthage. This calamity appears to have ruined the town; battered houses and overturned châlets remain as

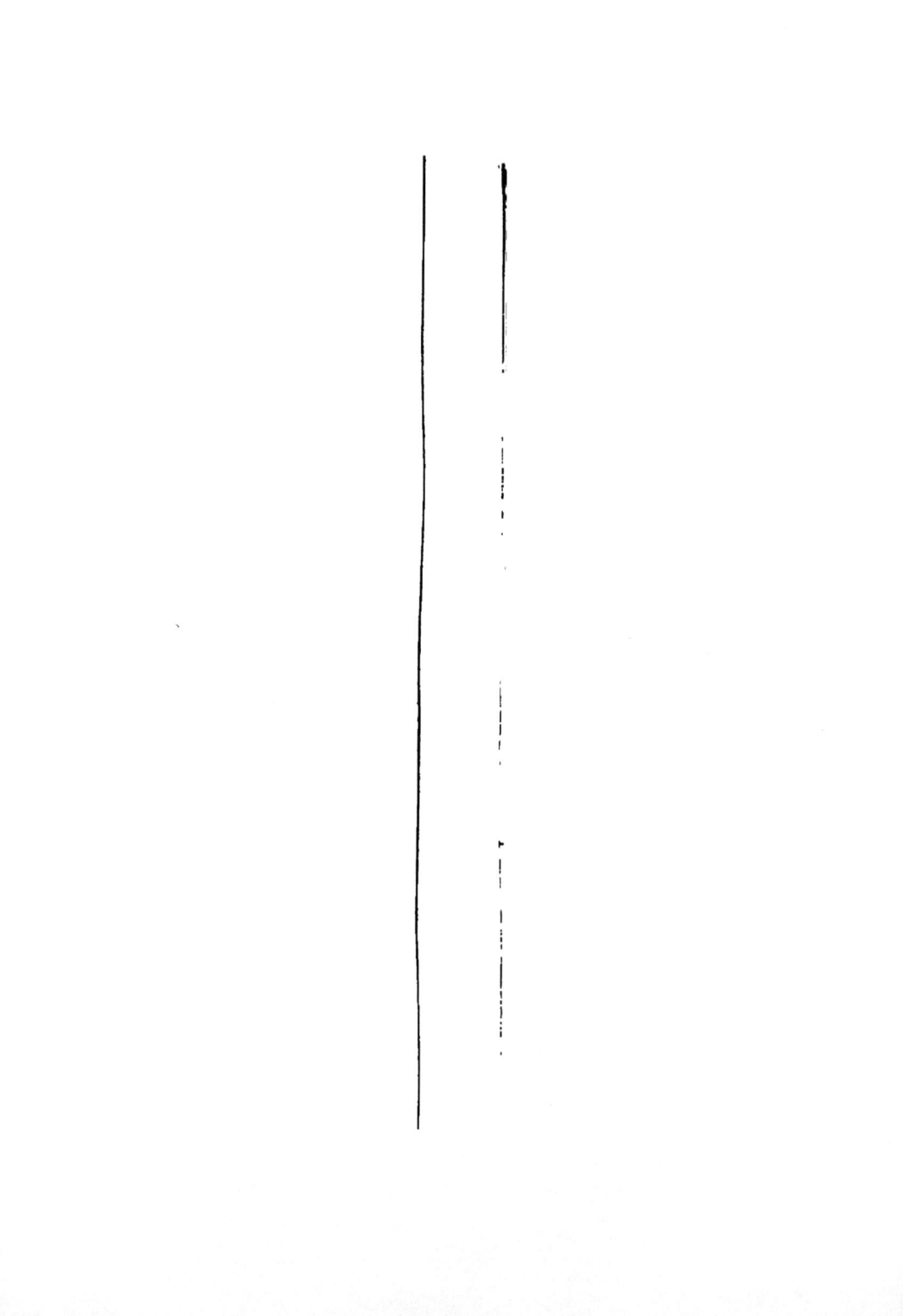

they were a year ago, from want of funds to repair them. Some of them have been set to rights, and great efforts are being made to repair the two churches, which suffered grievously; the whole interior of the roof of one had fallen, crushing everything in its way; railings, seats, organ-loft, and altar-steps, all had been destroyed, and the main walls cracked from top to bottom; the poverty of the place is so great, that a very long time will be required to restore it.

On the morning of the next day, the 28th, we started, with a prospect of fine weather, to walk up the valley of the Visp to Zermatt. A Prussian gentleman wished to join us, and ultimately, as we all got on very well together, he travelled in company with us for the next three weeks. The heat of the lower part of this valley is very considerable, and vines grow remarkably well; a capital white wine, with a delicious flavour of the Muscat grape, is made here, and at Stalden, about six miles from Visp, we only paid a franc per bottle for it. Two hours and a half brought us from that place to St. Nicolaus, which had suffered even more than Visp from the earthquake; while, strange to say, Stalden, which is exactly between them, escaped with very slight injury. The front of the Hôtel du Soleil, as one of the two diminutive inns is called, had been shaken out of its place, and the whole house rendered untenantable in 1855, but it had now recovered itself, and would have afforded a very tolerable sleeping-place if we had wanted one there. We walked on pretty briskly, with a magnificent view of the Breithorn towering over the head of the valley immediately in front of us, till we came to Randa, near which we halted by the side of a watercourse, to admire the magnificent Bies glacier which clings to the huge side of the Weisshorn, on the opposite side of the valley. I have never seen in the whole country so beautiful a view of a glacier without leaving the main track; the side of the mountain is so steep, and the road passes so close to its base, that the upper part of the ice seems at a most amazing height on looking up at it, and stretches across the deep blue sky in a succession of fantastic peaks and towers of the purest white. The foot of this glacier, like that of the Altels, is subject to periodical descents *en masse*, and on such occasions, happily at long intervals, causes frightful destruction in the valley below. In 1819, the mere wind caused by the rushing fall of ice and snow partially destroyed more than a hundred houses at Randa, and killed and injured many of the inhabitants.

A little beyond Täsch, the next village, the summit of the Matterhorn comes into view, looking down upon the valley with inconceivable majesty. We had been sitting down in a cool shady place soon after leaving Täsch, when I saw at the distance of about a hundred yards a figure advancing at a very rapid rate, evidently that of a swift-footed Mercury sent ahead by some other travellers with orders to pass us and secure rooms at Zermatt, which was understood to be rather full. This was a good opportunity of enjoying the amusement of a race, so I jumped to my feet in a moment and walked on as fast as I could. I arrived at the Hôtel du Mont Rose, and was warmly welcomed as an old friend by M. Seiler, who showed me our rooms, and had a chat with me; after which I walked quietly back towards my companions, who were following leisurely. About five minutes after getting clear of the village, I met my antagonist still walking very fast, and I was greatly amused at the comical expression of vexation with which he seemed to be pondering upon the fact of his having been so beaten in a four-mile course. When I met my two companions, they told me that, directly after passing them at our halting-place, he went off running, so they were rather agreeably surprised to find that he had not come up with me. After this, we all walked quietly up to M. Seiler's, where I was told that two of my former guides had already come to find me out, and presently I was shaking hands with Peter Taugwald and Aloys Jullen. They had both been with Dundas and me in many excursions in 1855, and in an attempt to ascend Monte Rosa, which failed in consequence of bad weather. We were very glad to meet again; and they wished to know what was to be done this year. I told them I hoped to succeed in reaching the top of Monte Rosa, but should wait a day or two for the chance of getting some one to join me in the expedition, as my own companions had no fancy for such an adventure. Meanwhile, it was arranged that Jullen should go with us next day to the Hörnli and Riffelberg, by a route which I had first tried in 1854, when we found it out for ourselves. We had on that occasion taken a guide up to the Schwartzen See, and certainly understood him to say, that he knew a way across the glaciers, and so round to the Riffel; but when we arrived at the gloomy tarn, we found that he had arrived at the limit of his knowledge; he could not even show us the way up the Hörnli. Under compulsion, but much against his will, he accompanied us while we discovered a way for ourselves: we had some fun with him, and promised to make a guide of him in time; but though he seemed rather nervous about the ice at first, he soon got on with a little coaxing. As he carried our dinner on his back, we could not dispense with his services, though he had engaged himself, as we considered, upon false pretences.

It was now arranged to go next morning by this route again to the Riffel; and as we intended to make a rather long day of it, Jullen was instructed to have a knapsack packed with provisions for a luncheon. After breakfast we started, and after crossing the stream, soon began to rise above the head of the valley: the path winds over pastures, with several châlets interspersed, and commands a fine view of the front of the great Gorner glacier, terminating below on the left. This glacier is now regularly advancing, and, from a point where we were no great distance above it, I could easily see, with the aid of a glass, that the ground was being completely ploughed up in front of it; indeed, there was no doubt that if anyone had had the patience to sit close by it all day, he would have seen a decided progress of the ice. The surface of the glacier, from its base to a considerable distance towards its source, is beautifully broken into fantastic pinnacles and blue caves, almost rivalling the Bossons at Chamonix, but not equal in exquisite purity and general whiteness. The Zmutt glacier was for the most part hidden by the high land upon our right, though it opened to the view when we arrived near the Schwartzen See. Nobody would ever go far to see this dismal little lake, were it not for the magnificent view in every direction from its immediate neighbourhood; there is, however, a chapel, scarcely so large as a small room, close to its brink, containing rough benches, so that it is to be supposed that on certain occasions a few peasants go there to perform their devotions.

From the lake we scrambled up some rough ground for a few hundred feet, and presently found ourselves on the moraine of part of the glacier which comes down from the base of the Matterhorn. That astonishing peak was immediately in front of us, rising with unutterable grandeur into the clear sky, with rather more whiteness than usual spread upon its tremendous precipices, in consequence of the recent falls of fresh snow. Other mountains are renowned for beauties of very various kinds, but the Matterhorn stands alone, the wonder of wonders, " an inaccessible obelisk of rock not a thousand feet lower than Mont Blanc!" We moved across a very dirty mixture of ice, *débris*, and half-melted snow, towards the line of the Hörnli, and soon found a place where

THE MATTERHORN.

we could scale its rocky and precipitous side. In a few minutes more we passed along the top of the ridge, and arrived at its extremity. This ridge is a long spur thrown forward from the base of the Matterhorn towards the Gorner glacier and Riffelberg, and forms a most admirable position for observing the grandeur of the whole vicinity of Zermatt. The amazing mass of snow, seamed with vast crevasses, which comes down from the Matterhorn towards the Zmutt glacier is far better seen from the Hörnli than elsewhere; and the general view includes all the giant peaks and vast glaciers which make a Cyclopean amphitheatre round the Riffelberg. The white top of the Cima di Jazzi, and the marvellous peak of the Matterhorn, are nearly the opposite points in a rough approximation to a circle which comprises in its circumference at least a dozen peaks of 14,000 feet, and upwards, in height.

After staying about half an hour to enjoy the view, we descended again to the Schwartzen See, near which our Prussian friend had been waiting in a snug corner. Thence a few minutes' walking brought us to the edge of the Furgge glacier; and looking out for a part pretty clear of crevasses, we soon crossed this very easy piece of ice, and began our scramble across the huge rocky region which separates it from the lower Theodule glacier. Our course was directly towards the Breithorn, and this, though quite out of the way of the Riffelberg, whither we were bound, is rendered necessary by circumstances of both rock and ice. The precipices that rise from the Gorner glacier are utterly intractable until a point opposite the Breithorn is reached, from which a descent can be made upon the Theodule glacier above its union with the Gorner; and even if this obstacle could be overcome by the most resolute scrambling, the glacier itself would remain quite impassable between the Hörnli and the Riffel. Accordingly, we made the best of our way over a rough and undulating line of rocky country for about two hours, keeping as close as we could to the lower edge of the great desert of snow and ice which covers the high land between the St. Theodule pass and the Matterhorn. Occasionally we crossed some of its more advanced portions, and close to the edge of one of these we put up a very fine hare, the first and only one I have seen at so great an elevation. In 1854 and 1855, I saw ptarmigan here, and they are not at all uncommon in wild rocky tracts among the snowy mountains. At length we reached the edge of this vast wilderness at the point which is arrived at in crossing the Theodule pass from the Riffel instead of from Zermatt. Here we halted a little to admire the vast glacier which, descending from the snow-beds between the Breithorn and Theodule pass, lay stretched out for an immense distance at several hundred feet below where we were standing. Between us and the Petit Mont Cervin, it was magnificently crevassed, the ice lying in huge white parapets one above the other. The Breithorn was full in front of us, and it was easy to see the course to be taken in making that ascent. The snows on its side towards us were too much broken to be practicable, but the way leads by the base of the Petit Mont Cervin, whence it winds up the end of the mountain which is turned towards the Val Tournanche. A friend of mine arrived at the top of the Breithorn by this way, in 1855, in only eight hours from Zermatt, and described the expedition as by no means difficult or dangerous. The ascent must be well worth making, for the Breithorn is an advanced post towards the south-west, and must command a beautiful view of the Piedmontese valleys in the direction of Aosta.

After a short stay, we descended to the glacier by a somewhat precipitous path, and began to move down the ice in a straight line for the Riffelberg. We had not gone far, when, by turning a little to the right, to avoid a rather tangled maze of crevasses, we came to a spot where, in 1854, as we were on our way to the Theodule pass, we had fallen in with the remains of a party who must have perished, in all probability, some years before. We found four or five shoes, such as are used by the peasantry, and many shreds of common blue woollen clothes, with the corner of a country knapsack sticking out of the ice, but the greater part of it was frozen in so hard, that without axes it would have been a work of considerable time to extricate it. The bones of the unhappy owners were completely whitened by exposure, and were spread about over a space of some twenty or thirty feet, mixed with others which could be easily recognised as having belonged to mules or horses. One man must have perished in a sitting posture; for his legs were covered by a thick pillar of ice which had formed around them, at the top of which was visible the place where the backbone and upper part of the body had in time been broken off from the lower extremities. Guides and all looked at this melancholy sight in perfect silence: no one knew anything of the lost party, nor had our guides ever heard of their bones being there. What a scene of suffering must have been here! The poor fellows had probably been overwhelmed by a snow-storm, in attempting to cross the Theodule pass, and died of exhaustion and cold, in struggling to fight their way through it. In 1855 I again saw these remains, but many of them had been carried away—as curiosities, I suppose—and in the next year very few were left to mark the scene of the catastrophe.

The glacier is remarkably smooth and easy to walk upon; the crevasses regular and well defined, and such as can generally be crossed with a good jump; but those who do not like to trust themselves in that fashion, find no difficulty in picking a way amongst them. Once upon a time, in making this same excursion, some of us found that a kind of steeple-chase over the firm ice, with crevasses to do duty as ditches, was highly exhilarating sport.

In due time we arrived at the moraine separating the glacier which we had been traversing from the Gorner, and having crossed this, we had a rather more difficult task to find our way amongst the huge undulations of the ice at this part of the latter glacier. The appearance was exactly as if the ocean had been suddenly turned into ice just after a storm, when the crested breakers give way to a rounded swell. Wave after wave, from twenty to forty feet high, succeeded one another in pretty regular order, separated from each other by shining white valleys, at the bottom of which was not unfrequently a pool of crystal water in a deep blue cavity. We threaded through, and, sometimes over, these for about half an hour, and then reached the moraine, which afforded a most disagreeable footing for some time longer: but it is necessary to follow it, as the precipitous rocks in which the Riffelberg here terminates are inaccessible. Lower down the glacier, we came to a point where we could leave the moraine and scramble without much difficulty to the high land of the Riffel. Our Prussian friend, who was out of health, had availed himself of a mule as far as the Schwartzen See in the morning, but he was by this time so completely exhausted, that I was obliged to support him all the rest of the way to the hotel. A week's residence, however, in that glorious air completely set him up again, and made him stronger than he had been for some months.

We arrived at the house in about nine hours from the time we left Zermatt; and, though the expedition might be easily accomplished in at least an hour less, yet it is so full of attractions at every point, that a little extra delay was fully made up for in gratification. To those who intend passing several days on the Riffelberg, this is certainly to be recommended as the best means of arriving there: if, however, only one day can be spared from Zermatt, it is perhaps better to go up by the regular path and proceed at once to the Gornergrat, which is the central point of the magnificent panorama.

To the true lover of the mountains this unpretending Hôtel du Riffel is the *beau idéal* of a residence. Surrounded by grandeur and sublimity, the traveller who takes up his abode there may spend many days in an endless variety of glacier and mountain excursions; or, if he feels in an idle humour, and prefers lounging on the grassy slopes of the Riffelberg, Mahomet may fancy that the mountains come to him without giving him the trouble of going to the mountains, so closely do they seem to approach on every side. The house has no pretensions to anything beyond plain comfort, but in the course of three visits I have always found every necessary requirement fully satisfied, and I have known at least one instance of ladies living there, as we did, for a week together, at the end of which they were greatly disappointed at being driven down by the necessities of time. The existence of such an inn upon such a lofty perch gives the neighbourhood of Zermatt a great advantage over that of Chamonix, supposing even we admit that the scenery of the latter is not inferior: its situation is about 7000 feet above the sea, and forms an excellent starting place for an expedition in any direction. The bracing air that plays across the down-like plateaux of the Riffelberg; the clear fresh mornings when the rising sun tinges the awful rocks of the Matterhorn with the deep red hues of the Tyrian purple; the calm evenings, when the vast snows of Monte Rosa repose "sunset-flushed" and glorying in the "golden air"; and the pleasant parties round a wood-fire in the little *salle à manger*, to talk over the various adventures of the past day — all combine to make a week's residence in this lonely spot a constant source of delight. The season for its enjoyment is, however, very brief, and the land around is more or less snowed-up for about eight months out of the twelve. From the middle of June to the middle of September, however, a fair share of good weather may be depended upon, though I must confess to having spent one or two days there without even a momentary chance of seeing anything at more than twenty or thirty yards from the house, till a break in the clouds about nightfall showed us the feeble light of the inn at Zermatt like a mundane star far below us in the valley.

Here then we had arrived; and after a conversation with M. Seiler, the landlord, in which I informed him my great object was to make another attempt at ascending Monte Rosa, and that I should be very glad to find a good companion like-minded with myself, we strolled out to the front of the house to enjoy the glories of the departing day. The sun had already sunk behind the Dent Blanche, but the great peaks around us were still glowing with a radiance denied to ourselves; the pure summits of the Lyskamm and the Breithorn were just tipped with a lovely rose colour, and the light behind the Matterhorn made the outline of that awful form stand out with peculiar distinctness. Far below on the right, lay the long valley of Zermatt with the tumbling roaring course of the Visp reduced by distance to a twisting silvery thread, and many a mile further still the well-known mountains of the Bernese Oberland rose serenely into the cloudless sky. Monte Rosa itself was hidden by the mass of the intervening Gornergrat, but my thoughts wandered to its summit, and an insuperable desire came over me to view the world around from the rocky pinnacle of the Höchste Spitze. With two friends I had made the attempt in 1855, but we were driven back by a snow-storm with intolerable cold before we had accomplished half the journey: the only revenge we obtained in the course of that day was a climb straight up the Gorner glacier to the Gornergrat, instead of following the long inclined path; we emerged on the crest of the

Gornergrat exactly at its highest point, and close to a party who had come up from the Riffelberg by the regular route. They were just seating themselves comfortably to enjoy the view, when they were suddenly startled at our appearance rising one after the other above the very steep parapet which extended from their feet to the glacier about two thousand feet below. After this the weather did not mend sufficiently to justify us in another attempt at the mountain, and we left Zermatt with a promise on my part to Taugwald, that if possible I would return the next year. Now therefore the time was come for the fulfilment of the implied part of my engagement: and while I was occupied in still watching the last light of day and meditating upon future possibilities, I was glad to find two young Englishmen had arrived from Macugnaga, having successfully passed the difficulties of the Weiss Thor.

We soon got into conversation together, and I found that they were as anxious as myself to make the ascent of Monte Rosa; but as they had just had rather a hard day's work, both they and their guides seemed disposed for a rest before making the attempt, and offered to start on Monday, after returning to the Riffelberg on Sunday. This being agreed upon, they started on their way down to Zermatt; but after a disappearance of very few minutes they returned, saying the weather was so fine that it was a pity to lose such a good chance; in short, they and their guides were ready to make the attempt the very next morning. This was pleasant news to me, and we soon set about making the needful arrangements. My chief guide, Peter Taugwald, was down at Zermatt, but I knew there would be plenty of time for him to come up before eleven o'clock at night, and in consequence of my former promise, I was determined not to go without him. My intended companions, Mr. R. Walters and Mr. C. Blomfield, had with them two capital guides in Johann and Stephan zum Taugwald, of Macugnaga. Jullen was also on the spot, and a very promising-looking young fellow named Peter Behren; and while a messenger was sent down for Peter Taugwald, we proceeded to hold a council of war in front of the inn. The Zum Taugwalds wanted us to take six guides and a porter: but this I firmly resisted as utterly unreasonable and not to be thought of; and, after an animated discussion, in which they contended for seven men, whilst I continued to declare that, on the occasion of our former attempt, Taugwald had said three guides were enough for three men, and that we had only started with three accordingly, the matter at issue was at last settled by a compromise, to the effect that we should take five guides and no porters; viz., Peter Taugwald, the two Zum Taugwalds, Peter Behren, and Aloys Jullen. I considered it highly important to resist the aggressive spirit of encroachment displayed in this matter: with all their good qualities, the Swiss have quite as sharp an eye for francs as most people; and if travellers are willing always to consent without a struggle to the terms proposed by guides, they may find themselves in the end subjected to the extortions of Chamonix.

This grand difficulty having been settled, we attended to M. Seiler's repeated assurance that dinner was getting cold, and repaired to the *salle à manger*, where we spent a pleasant evening in talking over our prospects for the morrow : the next thing was to give the guides proper instructions for laying in supplies, and then we turned into bed rather earlier than usual.

CHAP. VI.

An early Start. — A German Volunteer. — The first Rocks.—
"Look at Mont Blanc!"—The Old Route.—Severe Cold.—
A Difficult Crest. — Halt among the Rocks. — The last
Obstacle.—Astonishing View from the Summit.—A Trifling
Accident.—Return to the Riffel.

IT is very difficult to free the mind from all excitement on the evening before a grand expedition, and I had slept but very little when a tap at my door announced the presence of Jullen, who informed me it was half-past two o'clock, and left me about an inch of candle, which seems to be the customary allowance on these occasions, to insure getting up quickly. His brown face looked as good-humoured as usual, and yet for a moment I detested him as much as if he had been a gaoler come to lead me out for execution. This laziness, however, only lasted a few seconds, and I was soon dressed and down among the guides, who were bustling about in the passage, packing provisions, and making every preparation for the start. Nothing could be better than the weather; the whole sky was blazing with stars, larger and brighter than they appear through the dense atmosphere breathed by inhabitants of the lower parts of the earth. They seemed actually suspended from the dark vault of heaven, and their gentle light shed a fairy-like gleam over the snow-fields around the foot of the Matterhorn, which raised its stupendous pinnacle on high, penetrating to the heart of the Great Bear, and crowning itself with a diadem of his magnificent stars. Not a sound disturbed the deep tranquillity of the night, except the distant roar of streams which rush from the high plateau of the St. Theodule glacier, and fall headlong over precipitous rocks till they lose themselves in the mazes of the Gorner glacier. The breeze that played over the Riffelberg was scarcely perceptible, and all conspired to assure us of success in our undertaking.

After speaking a little to the guides, and inquiring if all was ready, I remounted to the *salle à manger*, and joined my companions, who were sitting down to hot toast and coffee by way of something comfortable to start upon. To my great surprise, I found with them a German gentleman whom we had observed in the house on the day before; he was now introduced to me as one who wished to accompany us to Monte Rosa, and as it appeared that he had a guide of his own, no objection to his joining the party was raised by our guides. We saluted one another, and he smiled most amiably, nodding his head with great vehemence to express his willingness to go through any amount of danger and suffering, no doubt; warned, however, by past experience, I had my own suspicions; the bare idea of a German attempting such an expedition was surprising enough, and I could not help feeling pretty sure that he would never reach the summit.

Time advanced, and the guides sent a message to say that everything was now ready; so down we went, and after a final look round, to see that nothing essential to success was left behind, our caravan of ten men started about twenty minutes to four o'clock, and began to move along the turfy path towards the Gornergrat, rising gently but steadily for about half an hour from the Riffel hotel; and, then turning sharply to the left, we followed a narrow track along the face of the exceedingly steep and lofty ridge which rises from the Gorner glacier till it culminates in the crest of the Gornergrat and Hochthäligrat. Never more than a foot wide, and sometimes consisting of mere notches in the solid rock, the path requires some caution in the darkness of the early morning, and would certainly be regarded with great suspicion by anyone who might find himself upon it for the first time under such circumstances; for if he were tripped up by a stone, he would probably have a roll down to the great glacier, about a thousand feet below. This continued for half an hour longer, during which our course descended gradually, till it met the glacier at a point where its side could be climbed up with greater ease than lower down. It is always, however, a matter of some difficulty for novices to scramble up a place of this kind. The edge of the glacier was rounded down towards us in an arch, and the early morning frost made the ice very slippery; the only way was to select with the eye the roughest part to be found, and then make a regular rush up it, never stopping long enough to make the balance of the body a matter of difficulty, or to give the foot time to slip. I believe our unfortunate German friend was not so well provided with nails in his shoes as he might have been; at all events, when I halted on the more level part of the glacier, and looked round to see how the others would come up, I saw him throwing his arms and legs about in the most reckless fashion, until he was successfully dragged up by the main force of his guide. Peter

A PROGNOSTICATION.

Taugwald's notions of him were, of course, not much higher after this display; and when, about a quarter of an hour later, I pointed out to him the poor fellow vainly labouring to keep up with us, but already far behind, he replied with his peculiar chuckling laugh, accompanied by the most mischievous of winks, "Platz genug für ihn darunter!" ("There is plenty of room for him down below!") Leaving him to his fate, we pushed along at a good pace over the glacier, which is at this part very easy to cross, being tolerably level, with few crevasses too wide for a practicable jump.

Meanwhile, the stars had been growing fainter and fainter, and the first streaks of light began to rise higher in the heavens, until, about half-past five, on happening to turn round, I called out to the others to look at the Matterhorn behind us, just touched by the rosy-fingered morning, and looking like a huge pyramid of beautiful fire rising out of the barren ocean of ice and rock around it. The suddenness of this glorious spectacle rooted us to the spot with admiration, and while we were yet watching it, the Breithorn on one side and the Dent Blanche on the other were illuminated by the same radiant glow. The intervening mass of Monte Rosa made it necessary for us to climb many hours before we could hope to see the sun himself, but the whole air soon grew warmer after the splendid birth of day. As we advanced, the mountain was full in front of us, and afforded abundant food for contemplation on the probable chances of success in our ascent. Difficult enough we knew it was, and I remembered that, in the summer of 1854, when Jean Tairraz by my side examined it carefully through a telescope, he shook his head as he folded up the glass, and pronounced the premature verdict of, " Non, Monsieur, c'est impossible; personne n'y montera pas!" Since then we knew the highest point had been several times reached, though many aspirants had returned discomfited, and all agreed in speaking of the last part of the ascent as excessively laborious. Then I thought of our own failure in the year before, by reason of a sudden change of the weather; but now the aspect of affairs was most promising; we were in capital condition, and felt confident of full success.

The next time I looked over my shoulder, I saw our German friend coming along at a fast pace, and smiling most benignantly as he came up with us: he then pointed to his feet with an air of triumph, and showed us a pair of *crampons* that either he or his guide had discovered in their traps, by the help of which instruments he had made up his lee-way. He was dressed in black, and as he took long, but somewhat waddling strides on these patten-like devices, he looked about as graceful as a black swan trying to get out of the way of the performances of the Skating Club. We were now nearly at the end of the first stage of our journey, and at six o'clock had crossed the glacier to the lower rocks at the base of Monte Rosa, at a place called Auf der Platte; where, before setting about the harder part of our work, we halted for a short time, and had some cold meat and wine by way of a second breakfast.

The rocks composing this lower group are very large and generally rather smooth slabs, which makes it a matter of difficulty to walk upon them; so we advanced up a gully or hollow filled with snow which intersects the group, and affords extremely good walking, though at a considerable incline; emerging from this we began to mount up a long bed of firm snow quite free from crevasses, and crisp with the morning frost; and at this point I observed on our left the only chamois seen in the course of the day; he was fully 400 yards from us, but even then did not seem quite satisfied with our appearance until he had cantered up the snow for some distance, and succeeded in establishing himself upon the top of some precipitous rocks whither none but a very bold hunter would have ventured to follow him. Soon after this the snow became much more steeply inclined, and so much broken that we were obliged to exercise some caution in picking a safe way through the numerous old crevasses, many of which were partly filled with fresh snow: and after passing to the right of the first two large groups of rocks, we turned to the left above them, and continued our course along a vast plain, which may perhaps be called the Grand Plateau of Monte Rosa, in a nearly northerly direction without ascending much for a considerable time, till, bending round again to the right to avoid a most dangerous and crevassed part of the snow, we commenced a long and steep climb which lasted for another hour or more.

Here the snow in front presented a tremendously precipitous wall from which the fresh blocks were evidently in the habit of falling constantly. Our direct course being thus stopped by an impassable barrier, we once more moved to the left, the route passing between enormous blocks which had probably fallen early in the season, as far as we could judge from their edges, already rounded by exposure to the sun. Taking care not to come within range of the most freshly fallen ice, where of course there was the greatest danger of more coming down at any minute, we moved on, gradually ascending until, as we approached a maze of gigantic snow crevasses, we were obliged again to turn to the right, and then began a long climb of sufficient steepness to make a zigzag course necessary. About this time, too, we found the advance of day was beginning to have its usual effect on the snow, and threatened to make the labour of ascending much greater than it had been yet: a halt was called, and snow-gaiters put on with due solemnity by all the party except my English friends, who were wearing boots already. The sun had by this time peeped over the edge of the mountain on our left front, making the snow at our feet glisten like a sea of diamonds, and compelling us to keep our veils down as much as possible. The pure sky overhead grew, as usual at these great altitudes, more and more deep and black, and, as Shelley says in " Queen Mab,"

> " The sun's unclouded orb
> Rolled through the black concave ;"

a fact which, in all probability, is as much owing to the violent contrast afforded by the world of snow around as to the increased purity of the air. In the laborious pull up this part of the mountain, Peter Taugwald, leading the van, made short halts after every few hundred yards, and, resting quietly and silently on his alpenstock, would turn round to review as it were his little regiment of followers, and carefully examine each countenance, to see how we were all getting on: not much was said by anyone on these occasions, for we knew we had plenty of work before us yet, but one of my companions hinted to me that Peter's frequent halts were owing to fatigue consequent upon the little rest he had had the night before. I thought I knew friend Peter better than that, and judged he was prudently anxious for us all to keep our wind and strength for the real difficulties which we had still to surmount. At one of these halts somebody called out in German, "Look at Mont Blanc!" and we were at once made aware of the very great height we had attained, by actually seeing the monarch of Chamonix and his attendant satellites right over the top of the Breithorn, itself at least 14,000 feet high!

Our field of view had for some time been rapidly extending: the Riffelberg and its highest points were already dim and indistinct in distance below us, and the Matterhorn itself had lost its wonderful isolation and surpassing height, backed up as it now was by peak after peak to the west of it, which, though shut out of sight at the level of the Riffel, now appeared soaring on high and nearly equalling those which in reality were much nearer. Nothing, however, was so startling as this sudden appearance of Mont Blanc, distant from us about sixty miles, and perched exactly on the crest of the huge Breithorn, which was only about half a dozen miles from where we stood. Anyone not accustomed to mountain views might have imagined it all part and parcel of the nearer range, but a second glance would discover the mistake; while a more experienced eye would at once detect the difference of colour which fixes the stamp of great distance on the snowy mountains;—a delicate shade of faint primrose colour takes the place of that pure white which distinguishes the nearer snows.

We now appeared to be about on a level with the Lyskamm, our nearest neighbour; and presently, after turning rather sharply to the left, and making a short but steep ascent, where the hardness of the ice made it necessary to cut steps carefully, we apparently came to the edge, if not the end, of all things, as precipice upon precipice led from our very feet to the torn and broken masses of the Monte Rosa glacier. From this begins the only route which has been followed with success to the actual summit of the Höchste Spitze. All the early attempts were made by taking a course which diverged from our route somewhat before where we now were, and led to the ridge which separates the highest point from the Nord End, whence the rocky side of the former was scaled. This last climb of 400 feet was always very severe work, for the rocks are almost perpendicular, and their clefts being generally full of ice, the cold endured by the hands was so great as to defeat the intentions of many a first-rate mountaineer. The Messrs. Smyth, in 1854, followed by Mr. Kennedy and several others, ascended by this route and were supposed to have reached the very highest point, till in 1855 Mr. Hudson tried the new route up the ridge which we were now going to ascend, instead of taking to the rocks on the northern side, and by that means was, as he says in an Appendix to a new edition of the "Ascent of Mont Blanc without Guides," the first who actually touched the highest summit of the mountain.

The ridge we had arrived at runs nearly east and west, and ascends at a very large angle: turning to the left, we began to ascend the steep ice, cutting steps all the way for a considerable distance, but keeping close to the edge of the precipice, so as to have the benefit of a sprinkling of snow a few inches wide which had accumulated there and afforded better footing than the ice. Peter Taugwald led the way, having fastened me next to him by the rope, Jullen being attached to the other end of it behind me. The rest of the party had a longer rope to themselves, and followed us at a short distance. Slowly and steadily we kept on our way over this dangerous part of the ascent, and I daresay it was fortunate for some of us that attention was distracted from the head by the paramount necessity of looking after the feet; for, while on the left the incline of ice was so steep that it would be impossible for any man to save himself in case of a slip, unless the others could hold him up, on the right we might drop a pebble from the hand over precipices of unknown extent down upon the tremendous glacier below.

Great caution, therefore, was absolutely necessary, and in this exposed situation we were attacked by all the fury of that grand enemy of aspirants to Monte Rosa — a severe and bitterly cold wind from the north. The fine powdery snow was driven past us in clouds, penetrating the interstices of our clothes, and the pieces of ice which flew from the blows of Peter's axe were whisked into the air, and then dashed over the precipice. We had quite enough to do to prevent ourselves from being served in the same ruthless fashion, and now and then, in the more violent gusts of wind, were glad to stick our alpenstocks into the ice, and hold on hard. Some of the party felt the cold very severely, as our position was much too critical to permit our adopting any of the usual tricks to promote circulation. Blomfield thought his hands were fairly frost-bitten, as they turned quite white, and were desperately painful. I had no gloves, and was obliged to tie up my hands in a handkerchief, giving them alternately the luxury of a little protection; but, do what we would, all were uncomfortable more or less while exposed to this biting wind, and when we came to a part of the ridge where a patch of rocks protruded above the snow and ice, it was unanimously resolved to get shelter under their lee, and wait there a little in the hope of the air becoming more warmed by the sun.

The drifted snow was lying thick and soft on our side of these rocks, and in all the clefts between them; but we soon found a passage through a kind of natural gateway, and carefully let ourselves down, one at a time, to a rough irregular ledge on the southern side; but, as there was not room for all the party upon this, some of us scrambled down a little lower to a somewhat similar shelf, so that the feet of the upper division dangled over our hats as we sat on the lower rocks with our feet almost hanging over the vast precipice, and looked at the wonderful view in front of and beneath us. What a change in a moment! Just before, we had with difficulty kept our feet against the attacks of a cold and raging wind, whose savage efforts had been directed towards blowing us over a precipice; and now we were in a dead calm with the accompaniment of a delightfully grilling sun, which soon made us feel as warm and comfortable as peaches on a south wall in the month of August.

Lapse of time and rough alternations of weather had broken off slabs of the slaty rock, which made capital seats, and we enjoyed a famous pic-nic on our airy perch with the provisions brought up by the guides, while the alpenstocks were stuck in a hole, and the ropes, now unfastened from our waists, were laid down beside them. Blomfield rubbed his nearly frost-bitten fingers with snow, and succeeded at last in bringing them to life again; but he declared that he had never felt such pain as the operations of both freezing and thawing. We all greatly enjoyed the warmth and shelter of our present position, and only regretted that none of us had any drawing materials to enable us to bring away even a rough sketch of the view in front towards the precipitous side of the Lyskamm.

At the end of half an hour we broke up our camp,

and, one by one, we got on our legs and prepared for the final battle to the summit. All knew that the rest of the work was no trifling matter, but I had not the least doubt of the pluck and determination of any of our party. Peter again tied me to himself at a distance of eight or ten feet, Jullen being the same distance behind me, and the others were to follow us in the same fashion as before. At this point, however, the courage of the German professor entirely evaporated, though he had done very fairly hitherto; and he declared his intention of waiting in shelter with his guide until our return from the summit, supposing we ever got so far, which he seemed to think rather doubtful. We did not waste much time in trying to persuade him to break his neck, and at once began to move forward without him, Peter expressing, by a knowing wink and a kind of snorting chuckle, his satisfaction at the verification of his morning's augury, that there was "plenty of room below." I have frequently observed that the best mountain guides look with great suspicion upon everybody except the English and their own countrymen in a mountaineering point of view: they distrust them from the beginning, and always seem maliciously glad when the grounds of their contempt are justified by the subsequent collapse of the luckless foreigner. They seldom take any trouble to cheer his fainting spirits, or offer him any assistance; and take delight in speaking of a difficult mountain as only good for Switzers and Englishmen. Possibly this may be partly "blarney," and possibly also because the English pay better than other people, Americans excepted; but certain it is, that of the swarms of French and Germans who frequent the main roads of Switzerland, and dawdle about in such places as Interlaken, it is very rare to find one willing to undertake a difficult day's work, and still more uncommon to find one who succeeds in it. On the only three occasions when I have been joined by Germans or Frenchmen at their own request, and with all the pretension of being able to do anything and everything, they all gave in before the chief difficulties began. One of these was a gigantic Frenchman whom I met at Zermatt in 1854; he bragged the whole evening about an ascent of the Wetterhorn, which I never heard of from any other quarter, and then volunteered to join us next day in an expedition to the Weiss Thor; but being frightened at the first symptoms of a morning mist, he implored us to return, and, finding us quite deaf to his remonstrances, withdrew himself and his guides, leaving us to finish a most pleasant and successful day by ourselves. So it was on the present occasion: the German *savant*, who really seemed a very good fellow, did not like the look of the remaining work before us, and seated himself as comfortably as he could in the snuggest corner of our late encampment; his guide reposed close to him, and we left them alone in their glory.

Up went Peter, followed by me and Jullen, and the others in the same order as before; and as we emerged from our shelter our feelings were, *parvis componere magna*, something like what I should imagine must be those of soldiers ordered out of the trenches to attack a fortress; rather a different sort of thing too; but in a small way we felt that we were going in for a sharp sort of struggle, and the enemy lost no time in opening fire upon us. The wind had increased rather than diminished; and, as head after head rose above our entrenchment, tremendous gusts drove the powdery snow into our faces with a violence that made us very glad to stand erect on our legs, and leave them to bear the brunt of it, where no harm could be done beyond a little tickling of the shins.

On looking about us we saw that our course would not ascend much at first, but we had to pass for a short time along a rough and irregular crest of rocks, here and there giving place to ice when there were large gaps or intervals between them, the general direction of this part of our route being a gradual incline upwards, which led to the base of the last cone. The whole of the ridge was exceedingly narrow, and the fall on each side desperately steep, but the ice in some of these intervals between the masses of rock assumed the form of a mere sharp edge, almost like a knife; these places, though not more than three or four short paces in length, looked uncommonly awkward; but, like the sword leading true believers to the gates of Paradise, they must needs be passed before we could attain to the summit of our ambition. These were in one or two places so narrow, that in stepping over them with toes well turned out for greater security, one end of the foot projected over the awful precipice on the right, while the other was on the beginning of the icy slope on the left, which was scarcely less steep than the rocks. On these occasions Peter would take my hand, and each of us stretching as far as we could, he was thus enabled to get a firm footing two paces or rather more from me, whence a spring would probably bring him to the rock on the other side: then, turning round, he called to me to come, and taking a couple of steps carefully, I was met at the third by his outstretched hand ready to clasp mine, and in a moment stood by his side. The others followed in much the same fashion. Once my right foot slipped on the side towards the precipice, but I threw out my left arm in a moment so that it caught the icy edge under my armpit as I fell, and supported me considerably; at the same instant I cast my eye down the side on which I had slipped, and contrived to plant my right foot on a piece of rock as large as a cricket ball, which chanced to protrude through the ice, on the very edge of the precipice. Being thus anchored fore and aft, as it were, I believe I could easily have recovered myself, even if I had been alone, though it must be confessed the situation would have been an awful one; as it was, however, a jerk from Peter settled the matter very soon, and I was on my legs all right in an instant. The rope is an immense help in places of this kind; and if every one of the party makes the best use of his wits, carefully watching every step of the man next him, and ready to give his support with the rope to the man behind him, this principle of mutual protection is quite enough to prevent almost any accident from becoming serious, and real danger ceases to be more than infinitesimally small, however alarming may be the appearance.

Whenever we stopped for a moment on a secure

piece of rock, and watched the approach of our companions, it was a curious sight to see them winding and twisting over the rugged way, one scrambling down the side of a rock, while another was pulling himself up the opposite side, and a third perhaps in the act of balancing himself across one of the ice-bridges which we had just before passed over.

At last we came to the end of this crest, and found ourselves at the base of our last difficulty. Fancy the dome of St. Paul's magnified to about five times its actual size, slightly flattened on the top, and converted by the hand of a magician into a compact mass of rock with a coating of ice and snow laid over it all except at the upper part, where jagged rocks protrude from the central substance through the icy crust. Fancy now a thin slice, broader at the bottom than at the top, where it becomes a mere rough edge, cut right out of the middle of the whole dome, and placed with the icy side towards you; and I believe you will have a tolerably faithful notion of the Höchste Spitze at the foot of which we now stood.

We at once began climbing up this, and Peter's axe was hard at work for the greater part of the way, though occasionally a little temporary difference of incline gave us a sprinkling of snow to assist our footing, but from the extreme general steepness these exceptions lasted only for a few steps. Having climbed to the top of this icy part of the cone, we came to the last crest of rocks, and here the alpenstocks were deposited in a cleft; for in the final scramble, we were to have both hands free, and to be ready to hold on by our eyelids, as the sailors say, if necessary. From this point we had about half an hour of climbing and scrambling as well as we could along an ascending and irregular ridge of disconnected rocks, something like that which we had already passed lower down, interspersed with occasional ice-bridges, but containing a few "mauvais pas" even worse than those below. Sometimes we had to crawl up a rocky parapet, and then let ourselves cautiously down on the other side of it, till, while our hands yet clung to the rough red rocks, we could feel our feet firmly on a ridge of snow or ice, which was then in its turn passed in a few firm but hasty steps, with all the care we could take to avoid a fall, where, if the fallen one could not be held up by the others, he would, in all probability, be dashed to pieces. I have, however, already alluded to "ifs" and possibilities, and beg leave to discard them entirely, considering, as I do, that with a properly conducted party of active men, the chances are

immeasurably in favour of a safe conclusion to any
excursion, however difficult or dangerous it may look.

Sometimes, when the rock in front was too perpendicular to climb over by any means without a ladder, we were obliged to scramble round it by the side, feeling with the toes for a ledge or a crack an inch or two in width, and searching for a similar convenience for the hands higher up. At last we came to a larger and deeper hollow than the rest, where we had to descend a rough rocky wall for not less than twenty feet, I should think. Peter, however, without the least hesitation or apparent difficulty, scrambled down this awkward-looking place, fitting the tips of my toes into the best cracks he could find as I came down next to him, while I performed the same service for Jullen who followed me. At the bottom was an ice-bridge; we crossed this, and then had a rough clamber for a few minutes up the opposite side of the gully. Taugwald is a surprisingly good climber; and though he is almost as broad as he is long, his great strength and activity carried him up places of this kind at a rate which, in spite of the advantage of long arms and legs, gave me quite enough to do to keep up with him; and Jullen, being no sort of match for him, was occasionally a great drag upon me. Directly he got even a few inches too far behind, of course I had the benefit of his weight upon my waist. In this last clamber up, his feet slipped when he was exactly under me, so that for a few moments I felt him hanging by the rope attached to my waist. Luckily, I had a good hold both with my hands and feet; so half laughing and half entreating, I shouted to Peter to stop a moment, while I helped poor Jullen to haul himself up and get a good footing: the whole work of the last hour had however considerably alarmed him, and his usually calm face looked more long and solemn than I should have thought possible. He had been with me on many a glacier expedition in the more immediate neighbourhood of Zermatt, and had always behaved like a good fellow: but he had never been as yet to the upper part of Monte Rosa, and seemed to find it more alarming than he had anticipated.

A few more scrambling steps, only a few feet higher, and we gave vent to a shout of triumph; for the object of our ambition was attained, and we stood on the highest point, the Allerhöchste Spitze, of Monte Rosa.

In a few minutes the rest of the party joined us, and then, guides and all, hat in hand, we let loose our full enthusiasm in a thundering cheer. The wind was still tremendously cutting, and it was impossible to remain long in the exposure of the topmost rocks, so we fell back upon our former tactics, and carefully crawling down a short distance towards the south, we established ourselves on the flattest rocks we could find, leaving the enemy to howl and dash himself against the stones over our heads, while we enjoyed the full warmth of an unclouded sun in perfect tranquillity.

Not a cloud defaced the gigantic panorama before us: the fair land of Italy commenced at our feet, and stretched far and far away till the view was only bounded by the obscurity of distance. Sitting at the very edge of the vast precipices which descend about 12,000 feet right down to the head of the Val d' Anzasca, we were at the end and extremity, as well as the summit, of the wild kingdom of rocks and snow; and a new world of verdure and cultivation was suddenly spread out before our eyes. The green plains of Lombardy and Sardinia, faintly tinged with blue by distance, and studded with innumerable towns and villages, some of which only looked like white specks of various sizes, fatigued the eye in the endeavour to comprehend their magnitude: all that we could do was to seize upon the most salient points of the picture, and fix them for ever on our minds.

Comparatively in the foreground were the lakes of Maggiore, Lugano, and Como; for though the head of the latter is eighty miles in a direct line from Monte Rosa, it was not even dimmed by the haziness of distance: all around these beautiful lakes was fresh and verdant; and, as we looked at the somewhat long and narrow pond which we knew to be Lago Maggiore, it was indeed difficult to believe that the journey down its lovely surface was in reality about as long as that from London to Brighton. Lower down, and seemingly but a short distance from the foot of the lakes, was a city in which we thought we could perceive a shining white mound that we felt to be what Tennyson calls " a mount of marble, a hundred spires " — the far-famed cathedral of Milan. Turning slowly to the right, the eye passed over an immense extent of seemingly plain country, and took in almost at a glance the whole continental possessions of the king of Sardinia, with the vast chain of Alps stretching from Mont Blanc to the Mediterranean. This chain presented a very beautiful serrated outline, in which the higher tops of Mont Cenis and Monte Viso were conspicuous, and terminated abruptly at the southern extremity on the edge of the sea. I could not distinctly assert that we really saw the Mediterranean, for the distance is so enormous that it becomes impossible to distinguish the horizontal line which separates the sky from the water: but judging from the perfect clearness with which we saw the very end of the Maritime Alps, and from the fact that the Apennines were not high enough to appear noticeable in the view, it is undoubtedly certain that our true horizon must have included part of the Gulf of Genoa, though the similarity of tint at so immense a distance made it impossible to say which was sky and which was water. Still turning farther to the right, a change came o'er the fashion of our dream: farewell to the fertile green and purple tinted plains of Italy! The Titans of the mountain world once more confront our sight; and here, close in front, separated from us by a vast gulf of snow crevassed into every fantastic variety of form, rises the nearest of them, the Lyskamm. Even while we were looking at it, there came the roar of a few hundreds of tons of ice thundering down its precipitious side, as if a great frozen giant had tumbled out of bed, and was waking the mountain echoes with his groaning.

A little beyond this came the Breithorn, now so much below us that we could look down upon its splendid white head, high over which Mont Blanc and all its dependencies were seen with perfect clearness, though the distance of sixty miles had so reduced the apparent size of this large group, that it was only just long enough to cover the summit of the nearer mountain. The Matterhorn had lost that unique grandeur of isolation which gives it so wonderful an appearance when seen from below, and was now backed up by countless peaks and glaciers of the almost untrodden land, only made known by Studer and Professor Forbes, which extends from the neighbourhood of Zermatt to that of St. Bernard and the Combin, beyond which again some of the highest summits of France were visible. The Gorner glacier with all its ramifications was laid out like a map beneath our feet as far as the Cervin pass and the foot of the Matterhorn; and scores of the smaller glaciers shone with nearly all the colours of the rainbow in their various beds, according as their position and inclination affected the dazzling light that fell upon them.

The rocks beneath whose shelter we were entrenched prevented us from seeing the view towards the north till we rose to our feet again; and then in an instant nearly the whole of Switzerland was added to the vast panorama! Near us, and only separated by a ridge, was the Nord end of Monte Rosa, the only one of the points which remains unscaled: but, though the last part of it would no doubt be very difficult, I should not think it is altogether unattainable. Further to the north, we had an admirable view of the two great ranges which enclose the valley of the Gorner Visp, that to the west culminating in the Weisshorn, and that to the east in the Dom or Grabenhorn, the highest point of the Mischabel. The last was, as far as we could judge, quite as high as the point we stood upon, and the slopes of rock and snow which lead to its sharp-pointed summit appeared to be inclined at so terribly steep an angle as to present a most formidable difficulty to the climber. The Weisshorn forms a magnificent star amid the constellation of mountains around Zermatt, and is about 15,000 feet high: seen from Monte Rosa its peak is remarkably like that of the Dom.

Far beyond these, and seen through a wide gap between the Dom and the Mittaghorn, shone the Jungfrau, queen of the Oberland, tinged with the same delicate yellowish shade that I had already observed on Mont Blanc: the Finsteraarhorn and many a well-known summit looked at us from afar like old friends; and yet further to the east, group after group of distant mountains, some of which must have been looking down upon the tranquil waters of Lucerne, were followed by the Tyrolese ranges, many of them far beyond the Ortler Spitze, where, at a distance of 200 miles, they displayed their snowy heads all tinged with a rosy light, though we had only arrived at the middle of the day. Thus we observed a regular gradation of colour on the snows, varying in proportion to their distance.

Such was the sublime view which we had the rare fortune to enjoy: rare indeed, as will readily be admitted by all who know the high passes leading down into Italy from the neighbourhood of Zermatt, and who must remember how often a climb of several hours has been repaid by nothing but the sight of an ocean of cloud and mist enveloping the whole of Piedmont, even when the weather might be perfectly fine and clear on the side of Switzerland. This had happened to me no less than six times; and so many old disappointments made the complete glory of the panorama from Monte Rosa doubly acceptable. I believe that one or other of our guides had been with most of the expeditions, both successful and unsuccessful, to this mountain, and they said the view had never but once been equal to that which we now saw.

We arrived on the summit about a quarter past twelve o'clock, and enjoyed ourselves there intensely for nearly three quarters of an hour. I had not felt the slightest sensation of fatigue, and I believe my friends were equally fortunate in that respect, though they had suffered more from the cold. None of us, excepting Behren, the youngest guide, felt any inconvenience from the rarefied air, though we were at an elevation which is stated by the last authority to be 15,284 feet. He had a slight cough at starting, which increased as we approached the summit, and perhaps helped to interfere with his breathing; but his bright merry eye showed clearly enough that there was not much the matter with him. Pipes were produced all round, and the concentrated smoke from eight happy and contented individuals might almost have been mistaken by an inhabitant of the lower world for the first symptoms of an eruption of a volcano in the Pennine Alps. Out flew a couple of corks, and we drank the Queen's health, besides that of each other and of the guides, with great enthusiasm: the latter did full justice to each toast, and cold winds, icy rocks, and other little difficulties were all forgotten in the exhilaration of the moment. We took good care, however, that the libations should be very moderate, as steady heads would be wanted for the descent.

We chipped off some pieces of the highest rocks, which contained a good deal of quartz, and about a few minutes before one o'clock began to prepare for the descent. We should have liked to spend another two hours at least on the summit, and it would not have been at all too long for a just and complete appreciation of all the view around us: all were very unwilling to leave the spot; but we knew that the first part of the descent would be rather a serious matter, and it would be advisable to allow a little extra daylight in the event of difficulty or delay. Accordingly, we got into our rope harness again, and started back in the same order as before, Peter Taugwald leading the way. In the scramble down the rocky crest, we followed as nearly as we could the course by which we had ascended; and hands, knees, and feet were in full operation whenever the surface gave us anything to hold on by. In about twenty minutes we reached the place where the alpenstocks had been laid by; and, not sorry to see them again, we prepared to descend the icy part of the last summit.

This was the most dangerous-looking part of the day's work: ascending it had required some steadiness, but as we stood at the top, looking down it, with all the immensity of precipitous depth close on each side of us, the prospect would have been rather a serious one for a nervous head. But down we must go: if we did not go that way, we must stay where we were, and accordingly Peter began moving down very cautiously, putting his feet sideways into the steps he had cut in the morning, and sometimes stooping to extend them when he thought them too small for security. Step by step I followed him with the greatest care, sometimes at a particularly bad place getting assistance from the point of his pole driven into the ice so as to guide my foot into the proper step, and then myself performing the same service for Jullen.

Having got firm footing at last on the rocks below, I could safely look round to see how the rest of the party were getting on; and nothing gave me such a striking notion of the nature of the slope which we had just descended, as the sight of my companions at the upper part of it, with their dark outlines standing out against the sky, and positively looking almost ready to fall upon our heads, if anything were to shake them off from their precarious footing. Hardly liking to look at them in such a situation, I turned away; but they all came down quite safely, and were soon by our side, after which we lost no time in passing the lower crest of rocks, and arriving at the place where our German friend and his guide had been waiting for us about two hours and a half. In spite even of the warm sun, they must have been suffering considerable discomfort, for their feet had of course been wetted through by the snow before they got there. At all events, they were glad enough to march off downwards again with us; for as they did not dare to leave the place alone, they had been most effectually imprisoned—chained, like Prometheus, to a rock.

We now began to descend the second grand slope of snow and ice. The greater part of it was perfectly hard, but a little fresh soft snow was still lying on the edge overhanging the precipices which led down to the Monte Rosa glacier on our left; and Peter, preferring this to the ice, kept, as in the morning, on the extremity of the ledge: it looked very dangerous certainly, but, except for the risk of giddiness, I am inclined to think that he was right: had he kept more away, he must have cut steps all the way down a long and very steep slope with an extensive crevasse at the bottom, ready to receive all waifs and strays. As we descended by the edge, we probed the snow with our poles before every step, and now and then we had to turn a little to the right on finding that they went completely through, and made a hole large enough to see the glacier at an enormous depth below.

When nearly at the bottom of this edge, we turned

fairly off to the right, and soon came to soft snow at a sufficiently gentle inclination to walk upon with comfort; we had passed to the left of the long crevasse, and, all difficulty being now over, Peter set up a shout of satisfaction, and then, intimating that we might play with the rest of the mountain, proposed to descend *en glissade.* He sat down on the snow, I sitting down close behind him with my legs spread outside his, so that he could hold my ankles: Jullen came behind me in the same fashion, I holding his feet, and off we started in the greatest glee for several hundred yards down the huge bed of snow in a few seconds, only stopping when the accumulations driven forward half smothered us, and fairly brought our train to a stand-still, amid shouts of laughter at the appearance we presented of animated snow-balls. As soon as we had shaken ourselves clear, and recovered our composure, we turned round to look for our companions: at first, they were not to be seen, and I felt for a moment rather alarmed; but presently they appeared over a hump in the ridge, already at a telescopic distance from us, and feeling their way down the edge where we had before passed so cautiously: they came very slowly over this part, and it was a considerable time before they joined us where we were waiting for them, but we then found that they had had a very narrow escape. It appeared that they had diverged a little from the course which we took along the edge, and getting to the right, found themselves on hard ice instead of the sprinkling of snow which we had made use of as far as we could. In this position one of the party slipped, and another fell over him, and nothing but a tremendous effort of strength and firmness on the part of Stephan zum Taugwald saved the whole party from an accident which might have been serious.

At length, however, they all joined us without any loss but that of an alpenstock, which had snapped in the course of the struggle, and we went on our way at a fast pace down the great snowy slopes which had taken so long to ascend in the morning. The snow was now soft, and we took long skating steps, each of which ploughed up a furrow for about a couple of yards: this was warm work, and presently, on making a turn to the left, which brought the sun full in our faces, we encountered a heat which was thoroughly scorching. This was partly owing to our rapid transition from the severe cold to which we had so long been exposed, and during which we had been prevented from moving fast enough for a free circulation; so that as we were now almost racing through the snow, with the full glare of the sun in our faces, and in a position sheltered from the wind, the heat for about an hour was almost intolerable. We doubled our veils over our eyes, and many of the guides had dark spectacles in addition, but we felt positively roasting; my hands burned as if they were being held close to a fire, and I was obliged to put them in my pockets for shelter, one at a time, so as to keep the other free for my alpenstock.

The snow, though soft, was very free from crevasses for the greater part of the descent, but, after a time, the streaked appearance of it gave notice of treachery. Peter produced the rope, and halted the party just as one of them went through up to his middle to prove the necessity of doing so. For about an hour we travelled in this fashion, without any adventure beyond an occasional slight break-through; but Peter went at such a rapid pace before me, with Jullen at a slower one behind, that I found myself nearly cut in two by the rope round my waist, which every moment grew tighter and tighter, till at last I was obliged to stop the train, and point out my ridiculous position to our leader. Poor Jullen was not in his best trim: he was tired, and seemed to have been regularly frightened on the upper part of the mountain. I had often noticed his anxious expression, and felt many a tug at the rope behind me in the course of the day; and when, during the latter part of the descent, I slapped him on the back, and asked how he found himself, he looked over his shoulder towards the summit which we had left, and, with a melancholy smile, said, he was very glad he could say he had once in his life been on the Höchste Spitze of Monte Rosa; pretty clearly implying, I thought, that he had no desire to repeat the adventure.

Soon after four o'clock, we arrived at the lowest bed of rocks near the junction of the mountain and the glacier; and here we halted, after our gallop, to finish off the remainder of the provisions, using for a table an immense flat rock, at the foot of which were some exquisite patches of bright blue gentians. We then followed the rocks a little further, till we found a good place for clambering over the moraine to the glacier: this we crossed rapidly, only stopping to examine some good specimens of glacier tables, which were spread about in great abundance; then leaving the ice finally, we made the best speed we could up the long sloping path to the foot of the Riffelhorn. A few minutes after six o'clock we arrived at the hotel amid the congratulations of our friends who had watched us with a telescope from the Gornergrat, and only left their post when they saw us fairly on the last glacier.

So ended this very successful expedition, the delights of which had far surpassed my expectations. Happily, there is no nonsensical fuss made about a mountain ascent at the Riffel, and there are no guns to fire, as at Chamonix, even if anyone wished to indulge in such an absurdity: but there was a pleasant and sociable circle of friends, with whom we concluded the evening very merrily.

Compared with the expense of ascending Mont Blanc from Chamonix, the cost of our expedition was very small. The guides at first tried for fifty francs each; but as they had only asked forty francs the year before, we resisted this demand on principle, and concluded a bargain for forty francs each and a good *trinkgelt* if we got to the top, and were satisfied with them: but in the end, we gave them 240 francs among the five. They behaved with great moderation in the matter of wine and provisions, and did not even take as much for the expedition as we had given them permission for. The German paid for himself; but the entire expenses of the day amounted, for our party of three, to only 12*l.*, and I never paid 4*l.* with such satisfaction in my life.

Mr. Kennedy compares the rivalry between Monte Rosa and Mont Blanc to the English wars of the Roses, and the world will probably be long divided in its opinion as to the relative merits of Zermatt and Chamonix: one thing, however, about which there can be no manner of doubt, is, the great advantage for mountain excursions afforded by the existence of the Riffel hotel, which obviates the necessity of passing a night in such an uncomfortable place as the hut on the Grands Mulets, or even the Montanvert, and reduces the ascent of Monte Rosa to an expedition which can be easily accomplished in about fifteen hours by a good mountaineer.

With respect to the comparative difficulty of ascending the two monarchs of the High Alps, both Mr. Kennedy and Mr. Hudson say that all those of their party who had arrived at both summits were agreed in considering the upper part of Monte Rosa far more difficult than any part of Mont Blanc, though the whole ascent of the former is, by the aid of the Riffel hotel, made much shorter than that of the latter. Till within an hour and a half of the summit, there is no particular difficulty about Monte Rosa, beyond the mere labour of a long and continuous ascent over the snow, and this is not thought much of by a practised walker: no one, however, should undertake the work of that last hour and a half unless he has previously satisfied himself that he can trust his head as well as his feet.

I consider that our guides were rather to blame in not recommending us to take more precautions against the cold : it is an enemy to which I believe that I am particularly impervious ; but had I known what the latter part of the ascent would be, I do not think I should have started without gloves, and something in the way of a wrapper to put over the thinnest of shooting-jackets. The attack of a north wind on that fearful crest is no trifling matter; and on Monte Rosa, which is peculiarly subject to this, one is apt to be powerfully reminded of Shakspeare's words : —

> "They that stand high have many winds to shake them,
> And when they fall they dash themselves to pieces."

CHAP. VII.

Attempt to cross the Weiss Thor. — Dangerous Snow. — Bad Weather. — An awkward Situation. — The St. Theodule Pass, or Matterjoch. — A fast Walk to Chatillon. — Ascent of the Cima di Jazzi. — Crevasse in the Nevé. — Effect of Clouds. — Symptoms of Winter.

IN the first week of September, 1854, I spent a day in visiting the top of the Weiss Thor pass and returning to the Riffel, as our intention then was to cross the pass of St. Theodule to Chatillon, instead of going to Macugnaga and Lago Maggiore: the weather was delightful, and though, as usual, there were mists on the Italian side, we had a far better chance of getting over the pass than I had upon the occasion of a subsequent attempt to do so. The next day we crossed the St. Theodule, or Matterjoch, arriving at Chatillon in less than eleven hours, and found the expedition, though long, much easier than we expected.

In 1855, Dundas and I paid a visit to the hut on the top of the St. Theodule, and started next day in

GLACIER BOOKS
MOUNTAINEERING & POLAR EXPLORATION SPECIALISTS

www.glacierbooks.com

SCOTLAND'S LARGEST SELECTION OF MOUNTAIN & POLAR TRAVEL BOOKS

- UK & Worldwide Climbing & Walking –
- Alps – Dolomites – Pyrenees –
- Himalayan & Asian Travel –
- Greenland – Spitsbergen –
- North & South America –
- The Greater Ranges –
- The Polar Regions –

- FREE Valuations -

- FREE Catalogues -

- FREE Booksearch On Any Subject -

- WE BUY BOOKS -

Browsers welcome,
please phone first

For helpful service, please contact Chris or Anne Bartle
Ard-Darach, Strathview Terrace, Pitlochry, PH16 5AT
Tel: +44 (0) 1796 470056   Email: info@glacierbooks.com

NEW, SECONDHAND & ANTIQUARIAN BOOKS

the hope of reaching Macugnaga by the Weiss Thor. We had two guides, one of whom was Peter Taugwald, and we were joined by two Oxford men who, having with them two more guides and a porter, swelled our party to nine persons in all. We left the Riffel inn about half-past four in the morning, with as fine a prospect of good weather as it was possible to desire. A day or two before, however, we had started for the summit of Monte Rosa under equally auspicious circumstances, but having been driven down by a snow-storm after four hours' absence, we had learnt the uncertainty of weather on the high mountains. Our party of nine arrived at the edge of the Gorner glacier, and were already on the ice when the astonishing glories of sunrise burst upon us; but the tinge on the mountain tops was too beautiful and too deep in colour to be quite satisfactory to those accustomed to such scenery. Still, however, not the smallest cloud appeared, and we had advanced across the *nevé* for more than an hour before an unpleasant-looking rim of low sulphureous clouds appeared on the further boundary of the vast fields of snow between Monte Rosa and the Cima di Jazzi. This was unpromising, but we yet hoped that, as the sun warmed the air, our enemy might quit the post which it occupied exactly in front of us. As we rose, we turned gradually away to the left till the view of the Findelen glacier appeared: the spectacle here beheld on turning round in the direction of the Riffelberg was sublime in the extreme, as, standing in the middle of the immense plateau of snow, we saw the two great glaciers extended below us and embracing the craggy sides of the Riffelberg which separates them. A vast crevasse, one of many, was close to us, in size and shape not unlike the chalk-pits on the South Down hills, but of a colour which ranged from a pale green on the upper part of the sides to an intense blue nearer the bottom, though we could form no idea of the depth: its greatest beauty, perhaps, consisted in a fringe of enormous icicles, some of them as large as the stems of young fir-trees, which hung down from the projecting edge of the glacier, shining with the same exquisite colours as the sides of the crevasse. Some of these monster crevasses extend for several hundred feet, and, being partly covered over with snow at the ends where their width is least, are not free from danger, and we had to pass a few insecure places. Even though tied together with a good rope, every one of us experienced a sensation described by nervous old women as "the creeps," when we felt all that part of the snow over which we were passing subside sensibly a few inches with a low harsh growl like the cracking of the ice on a pond. This happened twice; and at another time a very rash guide who came with our companions, and insisted on running forward sometimes by himself, was let through up to his neck, and only saved by keeping his arms stretched out till he was rescued by the others, who reprimanded him for his folly.

Meanwhile the ominous clouds boiled up higher and thicker than before, looking prepared to give us an inhospitable reception for our temerity in encroaching on their domains; and presently the foremost of them rushed down towards us preceded by a blast of cold wind, and a sprinkling of snow which rapidly thickened. Very shortly it became impossible to see anything at more than a few yards off, but still we persevered, hoping to be able, after taking our bearings, to keep the right course by observing the direction in which the wind blew. To add to our troubles, about this time one of the Oxford men, who had not had much experience of snow walking, became knocked up, and sat down to rest, much to the annoyance of the others, who minded fatigue much less than waiting about in such severe weather with nothing on their backs but the usual summer-clothing. We soon, however, advanced a little further, and then the porter professed himself to be incapable of further progress, and, hanging down his head, looked completely exhausted. A little brandy revived him, and again we moved on in single file, feeling very thankful that our feet made such deep impressions in the soft snow, that they would not be too much filled up to enable us to find our way back again if necessary.

We knew that we could not be far from the pass; and before long we came to the edge of the snow-field, upon which we halted to hold a council of war about its exact situation. We had by this time descended a little from the highest part of the snow, and the guides, after a short discussion, came to the conclusion that we were too much to the left; the snow on the edge in front of us seemed far from safe, so turning to the right, we kept a little away from it, and soon lost sight of it in the fog: we then continued rising, at first gradually, but soon very rapidly, through the snow, which admitted us at every step as far as the knee. Close to our left we could see a mass of long wreathing snow, which we knew was too dangerous to infringe upon, and for some time I devoted my attention to my footsteps; but at last, as I felt we must have ascended very considerably, I lifted up my head to try if it were possible to see any mark to direct us aright: the ascent we were making was so steep that I had to throw my head far back before I could see Taugwald and another man apparently balanced on the brim of my hat.

Just then the fog cleared for a moment in our immediate neighbourhood, and partly revealed to us the dangerous position we had arrived at. We had been climbing up the edge of the Cima di Jazzi! Not more than three or four feet from where we stood, the mass of snow wreathing in exquisite form hung over the side of precipices towards Macugnaga, the depth of which was still concealed by the mists below, while in front of us the edge of the mountain bending round to the left displayed a tremendous chasm, the sides of which were hung with monstrous green icicles, one row below another, until the lowest were veiled in impenetrable cloud. A more terribly dangerous-looking place I have never seen, even among these mountains; another step, and the whole mass of overhanging snow might have given way with our weight pressing close upon its edge!

This awfully beautiful vision, which for a moment had been permitted to "show our eyes and grieve our hearts" was in another moment withdrawn entirely: a fresh puff of wind drove another mass of fog towards us, and, without saying a word, every man turned cautiously round upon his steps and, holding hard by the rope, walked slowly down amid a silence which was not broken till we reached a place of safety. We were compelled to follow our old steps for fear of losing the only clue to guide our return by, and hurrying along to warm ourselves a little, soon arrived at a large excrescence of snow, under the lee of which we obtained some shelter from the wind, and accordingly determined to refresh ourselves with dinner. With this object we seated ourselves on the snow in a circle; but the seats were so soft, that sometimes one and sometimes another assumed a most ridiculous position by sinking down till his heels were nearly level with his head. We kept ourselves pretty right, though, upon the whole, and no one did more justice to the entertainment than the porter, who not long ago seemed almost at the gates of death. A slight lift of the mist now inspired with a new idea the guide who had distinguished himself more by his temerity than by his wisdom: he fancied he knew where we were, and that the pass was close to us; and Peter Taugwald being enticed into going with him, they took a rope and advanced to a new point of the crest which overhung the precipice; but in a few minutes they returned, having risked their necks, and found nothing. Under these circumstances it was considered that, discretion being the better part of valour, it was advisable to return at once. The guides were not agreed as to whether we were on the left or right of the pass; the snow still fell rapidly, and would soon entirely efface the already half choked footsteps, and the day was so far advanced that another attempt and failure would make us at all events very late for a return.

Accordingly we turned about, and, following our old track, arrived in about two hours at the lower level of the clouds: the sudden transition had a singular effect; for though we came out from our long battle with the fog and snow-storm all peppered with white, and garnished, as to the whiskers, with icicles, in a very short time heat became once more the predominant sensation; and as we arrived in the light of the sun, the skin began to burn and tingle as if we had been set on to roast at a slow fire. Soon after emerging from the cloudland, we came to a dangerous half-covered crevasse which had given us some trouble in the morning; with due care we soon passed it again, and were astonished to find an Englishman and a Swiss *savant* waiting there with a couple of guides. Apparently, they did not like to meddle with the crevasse, and were too much fatigued to return before they had enjoyed a rest; and on speaking to them, it came out that they had not left the Riffelberg till nearly noon, which was late enough to make their day's work one of difficulty, even if they had known anything of snow-walking. As it was, they were greatly fatigued; and, after many attempts to wait for them as we went homeward in company, it was found necessary to leave them behind us, and let them follow at their own pace.

A day or two afterwards we went up again to the hut on the St. Theodule pass, and crossed it to Chatillon: we found the hut in the possession of a very fine old man, who must be either the ghost or merely the successor of him who Mr. Wills has reason to think perished by some unfair means. Our friend was very busy about his house; and its situation, at more than eleven thousand feet high, did not seem at all to cool his satisfaction about it: he said he intended to have another room ready for the next season, and he promised to make the roof waterproof at the same time. He spoke French very fairly, having served in the army of Napoleon, under Marshal Junot; and his great pride now seemed to consist in having two sons in the army of the Crimea. We all drank success to the war; and then the Comte de St. Theodule, as he had been christened by us, went literally to a hole in the wall, which served him as a wine-cellar, being just large enough to hold a cask of about eight or nine gallons, and, drawing a large tumbler of cool and refreshing wine, he insisted upon our drinking its contents. We had a dull day for our excursion, and, there being no particular object in resting when there was little to see, we made the mere animal excitement of fast walking compensate for the more refined one of enjoying the grand scenery of this pass as I had formerly done. The dubious appearance of the morning had prevented our starting before eight o'clock; and in spite of nearly an hour's *séance* with the old man in his hut, and another hour's halt at the dirty inn of Val Tournanche, we succeeded in reaching Chatillon a little before seven in the evening, only two hours and three quarters having been occupied in ascending from the Riffel to the top of the pass. Peter Taugwald and Jullen were with us, and in consequence of the badness of the weather, we allowed them both to go on to Chatillon, so as to have the benefit of one another's society back to Zermatt; and it was quite amusing to see Jullen's face, as he wiped his forehead and declared he had never walked so fast in all his life. This is all very well, however, in walking down hill or upon pretty level ground; but in long steep ascents the true principle is one that Jean Tairraz told me:—"Plus on monte doucement, plus on arrive rapidement au sommet." The pass of the St. Theodule is interesting in the highest degree, and by no means difficult. The view from the summit comprises all the grandeur of the Zermatt scenery; and as the route bends round the shoulder of the Matterhorn, that magnificent summit is seen to the highest perfection. A long wild descent leads to the first symptoms of cultivation; and the gradual increase of richness in woods and pastures forms a perpetual attraction, which culminates in the approach to Chatillon. The path there winds along the sides of a noisy stream, sometimes over green meadows dotted with the autumn crocus, and sometimes through splendid natural woods of chestnut and walnut, growing among enormous moss-covered rocks, which have fallen long ago from the craggy mountains which skirt the valley, and in almost every cleft of which grows the dark and stately fir-tree. At last the white buildings of Chatillon appear amongst the green masses of wood, and the single arch of the old bridge seems to be thrown from the branches of one tree to those of another across the river that rushes over its rocky bed a hundred feet below.

This year, 1856, we had intended to cross the same pass again, with the view of being in time to spend a week or two in Dauphiné, after a visit to Chamonix. The Fates, however, decided otherwise. The day after the ascent of Monte Rosa, we roamed about the Riffelberg and Gornergrat, amusing ourselves with tracing the route with the telescope, while my brother occupied himself in making a sketch of the mountain. The next morning, at half-past four, we started for the Cima di Jazzi in lovely weather, accompanied for the day by a gentleman who, with his wife, stayed with us the whole week in Zermatt and the Riffel hotel. The route is precisely the same as that to the Weiss Thor, till the neighbourhood of that pass is reached, at the elevation of about 11,500 feet. The snow was in admirable condition, scarcely ever soft enough to admit the foot more than an inch, and it did not seem so much crevassed as in former years; we however crossed the narrow end of one huge crevasse, which extended for many hundred feet across the glacier, and was at least fifty or sixty feet wide in the middle, where it had the appearance of a vast blue cavern fringed with icicles. Turning here to the left, we skirted the upper edge of this at a respectful distance; and, as the glacier was steeply inclined down towards it, we thought it prudent to make use of the rope for fear of an accident. After passing for several miles over the great snowfield, we found ourselves at the level of the Weiss Thor; and, turning to the right, began to ascend the white cone of the Cima di Jazzi. The incline is steep, but not excessively so, and in half an hour we stood on the top. There was all the usual excitement of — "Shall we see Italy?" But the mystery was soon solved in what, I must say, is the usual manner: though we had not yet seen the smallest mist, the first step on the summit showed us an ocean of white rounded clouds, veiling everything, from Macugnaga at our feet, to the distant plains of Lombardy. A very beautiful effect was produced by the tops of the Monte Moro, and a few other high mountains in that direction, standing out in the bright sunshine like islands in a snow-white sea. Every now and then a light cloud made a vigorous effort to overtop the summit of the Cima, and surround us with a cold embrace, but a fresh breeze blowing from the north-west always caught the intruder and flung him down the precipice; and as he wrathfully curled and twisted about, it was curious to watch the effects of disappointed ambition. The whole view of the Swiss side was still perfectly clear, and the many peaks of Monte Rosa, now in close proximity to us, were shining brilliantly in the blue sky. The Gorner and Findelen glaciers could be traced for the greater part of their length; and far away were the many summits of that almost unknown land between Zermatt and the Grand St. Bernard.

We seated ourselves as well as we could, and proceeded to luncheon; but the cold was considerable, and most of the party were rather glad to take to their feet again and begin a rapid descent. Throughout the greater part of the return the sun was nearly in front of us, and the glare of its reflection from the snow was so excessive, that, in spite of veils, we were a good deal scorched, and next morning our puffed faces presented a very ridiculous appearance. The expedition was, however, a very delightful one, and as the summit may be easily reached in four hours and a half, it is not at all too much for a comfortable day's work. Near the foot of the Höchthäligrat a little water trickles down among the rocks, and there I saw the lovely deep blue gentians growing in solid masses of blossom, some of them at least a foot in diameter. The rocks at the foot of Monte Rosa are equally prolific in these turquoises of the vegetable kingdom, and I have nowhere else seen them in such profusion.

Another day was spent upon the sketch of Monte Rosa and in flower-hunting; but the cold weather came on apace, and in the afternoon, even where the sun was still shining, the colours froze upon the paper. The next day we were surrounded by a thick cold mist, followed in the afternoon by a heavy shower of snow; but the night was brilliantly clear, with a sharp frost, which completely whitened the Riffelberg in the morning; and several guides who were in the house declared that it would be dangerous to attempt the pass of St. Theodule on account of the risk of frost-bites. Peter Taugwald, ever the boldest, said he had no objection to go, but the voice of the majority was against the proceeding; so we made up our minds to bid adieu to the Riffelberg, and descend to Zermatt, Stalden, and Saas, with the view of crossing the Monte Moro to Macugnaga on the following day.

Before quitting the neighbourhood of the Riffel, I ought to say, that I have nowhere seen anything of its kind to compare with the astonishing grandeur of the vast plateau of snow at the head of the Gorner and Findelen glaciers, which extends from Monte Rosa as far as the Strahlhorn in one direction, and from the Riffelberg to the Cima di Jazzi in the other, covering many square miles with a robe of unspotted whiteness, which must be many hundreds of feet thick. The only variation of colour is to be found in the enormous blue crevasses, of the depth of which I have never been able to form any estimate, as the masses of snow overhanging their edges, and terminating in fringes of gigantic icicles, make it extremely dangerous to attempt a close inspection of their recesses. One is compelled to keep a respectful distance, with a vague idea of their having no bottom whatever. Here, too, I have often observed that, under a clouded sky of a colour like lead, a hole made about a foot deep by the alpenstock presents an appearance of the purest blue, which, at all events, cannot be referred to any effects of reflection, and must remain for the present a mystery to the scientific world.

CHAP. VIII.

Farewell to the Riffel. — Stalden. — The Valley of Saas. — M. Imseng, the Mountaineering Curé. — The Allelein Glacier. — Pass of the Monte Moro to Macugnaga. — Lochmatter "at Home." — The Val d'Anzasca. — Ponte Grande. — Feriolo. — Lago Maggiore.

SOME time had been wasted before we determined to leave the Riffel and go to Saas, and, in truth, the change of plan was attended with some difficulties, the guides having come up to the Riffel under orders for the St. Theodule pass, and we being no longer willing to go with them. For my own part, I was always ready to go wherever Peter Taugwald considered we might venture safely, but some of our party might possibly have suffered from the cold; and, as Ulrich Lauener chanced to be on the Riffel, and gave his very decided opinion against the propriety of crossing the pass, we at last all agreed in at once marching down to Zermatt.

About seven o'clock we started among the most

kindly farewells of all the little establishment, and were very glad to warm ourselves by running down when the nature of the ground permitted. The morning was excessively cold, the path as hard as ice, and a thick rime-frost covered all around us. As the white morning fog cleared away, the Matterhorn again stood forth in full beauty, thoroughly whitened by the recent bad weather and heavy snows, but a huge blanket of mist still rolled over all the neighbourhood of the pass we had intended to cross, and showed clearly enough that we should have had a very dreary and inhospitable reception. The greater part of the mule-road down to Zermatt lies through a forest of pines, some of them very large, with a great variety of shrubs and smaller plants and flowers growing between them. Sometimes this wood is thick enough to form a complete screen, and then again emerging for a little into a more open space, we see the winding curve of the Gorner glacier on our left as it sweeps down to its present boundary, close to the green meadows of Zermatt itself. Already in its onward march it has attacked and driven in some of the outposts, and if its advance continues as rapidly as of late for many seasons longer, the damage to property will be very severely felt by the poor inhabitants of the village.

We soon left the picturesque woods behind us, and found ourselves following a narrow path among the meadows, which were covered with frost, even as low down as Zermatt; and, hurrying along in the certainty of a very long walk before night, we arrived at the Hôtel du Mont Rose after a descent of about an hour and a quarter from the Riffel. Here a mule was at once ordered out to take charge of the Prussian and his baggage, which was somewhat ponderous for the mountains; and while this was being prepared, I contrived to arrange matters with our guides, who had seemed disappointed at losing their expedition over the pass. In a few minutes more we were ready, and moved down the valley. The man who owned the mule wanted to put up at St. Nicolaus for the mid-day halt, but as we were to go to Saas in the course of the day, this was considered a bad division, as it would leave so much to be done in the evening: a small bribe induced him to defer to our opinion, and the whole party pushed on to Stalden without stopping more than a few minutes.

This had been a long stage of twenty-three or twenty-four miles from Zermatt, besides the descent from the Riffelberg, and both man and beast were fully prepared for a meal. A little before four in the afternoon we star ed for Saas, where we arrived about seven, when it was too dark to see much of the neighbourhood. As long as the light lasted, we had ample opportunity for deciding that the valley of Saas is far more picturesque than that which leads to Zermatt, the latter being more stiff and bare, with the exception of some fine scenes near Täsch and Randa.

The evening effects had been most beautiful for the last hour or two, and the mountains on our left were illuminated by the setting sun long after we had been left in gloom; but by the time of our arrival at the good curé's house, darkness reigned all around the valley, so that after our walk of about forty-two miles, we were all rather glad of bright lights and a good fire preparatory to a capital plain supper, of which real chamois formed an important element. The only strangers in Saas besides ourselves were three or four young Englishmen, who had come over the Monte Moro, and having, I suppose, never seen a really difficult mountain pass, were treating us to a very exaggerated account of their own exertions. They seemed, however, to be fatigued, and, soon after supper, left us comfortable enough in the possession of the *salle à manger,* where we had some conversation with the curé's second in command, a remarkably strong active fellow, who had, a few days before our arrival, made the first ascent of the Alleleinhorn, in company with the same friend of mine who had previously attempted the Finsteraarhorn.

I should have very much liked to stay several days at Saas, to visit the Fée glacier, and some of the wonders of the Mischabelhörner; but as our plan was now completely changed, and the journey round the south side of the Pennine Alps must needs be completed before seeing Chamonix, there was no time to be lost, and next day the pass of Monte Moro must be crossed to Macugnaga, in spite of the last travellers' account, which represented it as covered with ice and full of difficulty.

The morning was not so frosty as that of the day before, and the weather generally fine; but a mass of cloud seemed to hang about the tops of the mountains in front of us, which did not augur well. As the upper part of the pass was reported impracticable for the mule, it was arranged that the Prussian should ride as far as his beast could go, and from that point the baggage was to be carried by two porters to Macugnaga. One of these was a stout jolly fellow, and the other was a woman, the wife of M. Imseng's man-cook.

From De Saussure's time, downwards, it has been remarked, that near Saas the women are willing to do far more than the men; in short, that "the grey mare is the better horse;" and certainly our lady-porter did her work admirably, skipping up and down really difficult places with a very heavy load, at a pace which would have made it difficult for the best of walkers to keep up with her, though perfectly free and unburdened.

M. Imseng, the curé, showed us with great pleasure the silver snuff-box presented to him by Mr. Wills and Mr. Heath, and pointed with satisfaction to the inscription in Latin, and especially the words "per nives sempiternas et rupes tremendas," reading which he seemed to fire up like an old war-horse. A most excellent man he seems to be in his village, and universally esteemed; but it is, of course, quite impossible for a priest, in so poor and secluded a valley, to keep up the appearance and gentility which is expected in the clergymen of town life; at all events, if anyone expects much in this way of M. Imseng, he will be disappointed. He is well-known, however, as a most excellent mountaineer, and, though between sixty and seventy years of age, can hardly be surpassed by the youngest in that capacity; all who have had the advantage of his company on difficult expeditions, speak of him in the warmest terms of gratitude.

As we parted from him in the morning, he said, he hoped we should return another year, earlier in the season, and see more of the neighbourhood, adding, with a laugh, and pointing his finger to some of the lofty peaks around, that there were several snowy giants as yet unscaled by foot of man, in an attack upon which he should be very happy to join. Farewell, then, for the present, to Saas and its simple pastor; but we hope to meet again.

After leaving the village, the path became rapidly worse; winding along by the side of the eastern branch of the Visp, it frequently became indistinct, and occasionally invisible, where the encroachments of the vicious little river seemed to have washed over it in rainy weather and the vernal meltings of the snow; and presently we crossed the noisy torrent over a bridge, which, consisting only of a couple of planks, and approached by two or three high steps, was a sufficiently awkward place to take a four-footed beast over, but our Prussian friend's mule seemed to treat it quite as a matter of course, and was soon safe on the other side. The great icy barrier of the Allelein glacier was now in front of us, completely filling up the valley, and making it a matter of wonder how the road could pass it. In its front was a large cavern in the ice, out of which rushed the stream of the Visp, having made its way completely under the glacier from the lake above it that is formed by the partial damming up of the waters which descend from the great glaciers in the vicinity of the Moro and the Rothhorn, the Strahlhorn and Alleleinhorn. Just in front of the foot of the glacier the surface of the valley was still covered by the black remains of an enormous alavanche of snow which had fallen in the early part of the season, bringing down with it a vast amount of vegetable matter and soil from the sides of the mountain on the left: making our way through this scene of ruin, we found the path turn to the left, ascending rapidly for a short time till we were on a level with the surface of the glacier, crossing which we were in a few minutes on the bank of the Mattmark See, a desolate lake, whose waters, ruffled by a fresh wind from the south, were dashing in waves against the lofty pinnacles of blue and green ice which formed its boundary, and rose above its surface in a most fantastic variety of form.

A remarkably bad path leads from this point to the Distel Alp, where a new house has just been built, but not yet properly opened. Here we were to get some provisions to carry forward for luncheon at the top of the pass, and on entering found a few inhabitants in the only room that seemed habitable. Upon inquiring, we found that they had plenty of eggs and cheese, and one of the women began to select a quantity of the former by plunging several dozens in a tub of water, and rejecting all those which, by floating, were, like witches, proved to be undeniably bad. The rest were boiled hard, and packed up with some cheese; after which we went on our way, the path becoming worse every minute, and generally consisting of heaps of stones about as agreeable to walk over as a Parisian barricade. The last châlets, which were of a most filthy description, were passed, and an ascent of about half an hour brought us upon a kind of plateau, ornamented with a vast quantity of ranunculuses, beyond which it was declared that the mule could not proceed.

The beast and his owner were accordingly dismissed, and we set about the last climb. In front of us was the Rosswang glacier, which we passed on our left, mounting over a very rugged way, every moment drawing nearer to the raw cloud which covered the upper part of the pass, and which we knew would soon receive us in its cold embrace. A great quantity of water continually trickles down the rocks on the right, and the severe frost of the last few nights had formed it into long rows of beautiful icicles, rising one above the other, and fringing every edge of the precipitous sides with perfect corridors. The effect of this was charming; but we were compelled to be careful as we admired it, for every stone we stepped upon was from the same cause coated with fresh ice, and of course very slippery. Here and there the regularly paved appearance of the path seemed to show that it must formerly have been far more generally used, and probably by beasts of burden as well as mankind; but in all likelihood the snow has been encroaching.

Before we got to the top, we plunged into a thick raw mist of the most uncomfortable description, and were obliged now and then to halt, so as to prevent the rear of the party from losing sight of the van. Climbing over a bed of snow at a considerable incline, we at last found ourselves at the cross which marks the summit of the pass, in about four hours from Saas; and here we overtook a man walking leisurely along by himself. The wind was cold and severe, so we descended the south side a little way to get under the shelter of some lofty rocks, where we prepared for lunch, and invited the stranger to join us. To my great surprise, he declined, and passed on in the same quiet way as before, anxiously looking about him. In a quarter of an hour the mystery was solved by the appearance of several men who had followed us, each of them carrying a large bale of goods on his back, and steadily following the course over the snow taken by the first man. Our porter explained that this was a party of smugglers working their way over into Italy, the first man acting as a sort of pilot-fish to see whether the way was clear.

The state of the weather was disagreeable enough in itself, but the most vexatious feature of the case was that the dense mist entirely shut out from our sight the magnificent view of Monte Rosa, which ought to have greeted our arrival upon the summit of the pass. As we descended the southern side, we soon got clear of actual contact with our foggy enemy, but the clouds were in dense piles above us in every direction, and we were deprived for the day of that which is universally admitted to be one of the grandest sights in Europe. The only solace on our way down was a very vulgar one, in the shape of immense beds of the shining dark whortleberry, upon which we regaled ourselves with great satisfaction.

After a charming walk down through the woods, we arrived at Macugnaga early in the afternoon, in little more than half the time which our friend of the day before had foretold would be necessary, and yet we had not at all hurried ourselves. We at once betook ourselves to Lochmatter's house, which is devoted to the entertainment of man and beast, and found the worthy owner engaged, like Cincinnatus, in the cultivation of his little garden. He was overjoyed to see us, as we had met on the Riffelberg a week before, when he had expressed himself as extremely anxious to form one of our party for Monte Rosa; and, when I found what an unusually good fellow he was, I could not help feeling very sorry that, for the sake of fifty francs, we had not indulged his wish. Lochmatter is one of the very best men of his class that I have ever met; active as a deer, he makes himself extremely agreeable, and is full of intelligence, besides having the great advantage of speaking French; and I should very much wish to spend a week with him, for the purpose of hunting the Mischabelhörner together, and crossing the Weiss Thor, for which pass no better guide can be found. He is passionately fond of chamois hunting, and entertained us all the evening after supper with accounts of his favourite sport, and his vain endeavours to fall in with a *bouquetin*, which he seemed to despair of; though he added, that he intended once more to search the dreadful recesses of the great Grabenhorn or Dom, where he thought the only chance remained. Though his house is a mere rough châlet, without even proper fastenings to the doors, he contrived to make us thoroughly comfortable by his watchful attendance to all our wishes.

In the afternoon he volunteered to take us to see the church; and it was really surprising to see that, in a miserable little scattered village like Macugnaga, the aggregate value of which could not be equal to that of one handsome house in London, the good Catholics had contrived to collect in their church an amount of ornaments and treasures that would have done credit to many a respectable town.

Rain fell heavily in the evening, and though this had ceased in the morning, the higher parts of the view were enveloped in clouds, and nothing could be seen of Monte Rosa or the Pizzo Bianco. We could not, however, wait for a change, and, greatly disappointed, were obliged to start down the magnificent Val Anzasca. Near La Burca we met a man who was very anxious to sell us a fine bird which he had just killed, and which seemed to be exactly the same as our grey hen. We afterwards heard that there was a considerable quantity of black game and partridges in the neighbourhood, besides a few pheasants. Our path lay close to the river Anza, which springs from the glaciers of Macugnaga, and finds its way down to the Lago Maggiore through a valley surpassing in beauty and magnificence any that I have seen, even though the dulness of the day, and the clouds which still hung about the mountains, prevented our seeing it to advantage.

After passing a few picturesque mining-stations, where a small supply of gold is obtained, we soon left the wild regions behind us, and followed the winding path among splendid chestnut and walnut trees, now and then coming upon a pretty village, thoroughly Italian in character, the inhabitants of which had availed themselves of every suitable piece of wall to ornament it with paintings in fresco. Trellised vines hung about the houses, and on both sides of the valley the hills were covered with almost every species of tree to their very summits. All these beauties seemed to culminate in Ponte Grande, where a side valley towards the south opened up a fresh variety of loveliness by breaking the somewhat monotonous regularity of the Val Anzasca. We arrived there about noon; and as a carriage road leads from that point down to

Vogogna on the Simplon road, we ordered out a vehicle whilst we proceeded to luncheon.

The first symptom of our being within the reach of Italian imposition was, that the landlord came forward to assure us, with the deepest regret, that there was not a single horse or mule to be got in Ponte Grande, in consequence of a neighbouring fair or festival; he had plenty of *voitures*, and it was so unfortunate that we should not be able to proceed! His statement was corroborated by a courier in the service of an English *milord*, who assured us that his master, who turned out to be one of the highest judges in our land, was "cribbed, cabined, and confined" for the same reason. We thought that possibly the courier was in league with the innkeeper, and made up our minds to try another plan. So we sent for our porter, who had accompanied us from Saas, and, informing him of the state of the case, offered him an extra franc if he could find us a horse. This succeeded admirably: in a few minutes he returned, saying he had found a horse, which would be ready very shortly. The landlord seemed considerably disgusted at this turn of affairs, for he had looked upon our party as safe for the night; but most of the inhabitants were, I fancy, rather amused, and as one man brought up the horse, several others began to make themselves useful in tying up springs and repairing harness. Before long we were off, baggage and all, in an open four-wheeled fly, and went rapidly along the gradually descending road towards Vogogna. This road is carried along the side of a rather precipitous range of hills, and overlooks the gorge of the Anza, far below; so far below, that sometimes, though you may see the white foam breaking upon its rocky bed, the roaring sound is inaudible.

There were many signs of the fall of large stones and rocks from the upper part of the mountains that overhang the road, under which, indeed, it is occasionally tunnelled through the solid rock; and at one place we saw, at a great depth below us, a house, which had lately been entirely demolished by the fall of a huge rock, nearly as large as the Bowder stone near Derwentwater, which had rolled down from the heights and dashed it to pieces, meeting, however, with just sufficient resistance to check its progress, and stop it in the middle of the ruins. In the course of our descent, our trumpery rope harness became seriously disarranged, and we lost our wooden drag on the first occasion of its application, after which it was ludicrous to see the anxious face with which our driver entreated us to get out at every difficult part of the road, and spare himself and his conveniency from destruction.

In due time, however, we safely arrived at Vogogna, and pulled up in front of the Post Hotel, as our Ponte Grande *voiturier* refused to have anything more to do with us. We at once commenced driving a bargain for a carriage to Feriolo on the Lago Maggiore, and began with assuring the master that we must positively go somehow, and should walk if he did not come to satisfactory terms. He and his people were very civil, and soon produced a rather grand-looking *voiture* from the *remise*, and a tolerably satisfactory arrangement was concluded. However, as usual, the carriage required a good deal of looking to, and whilst sundry screws and springs were put to rights, we were regaled with plenty of ripe grapes and peaches from the wall of the inn-yard, which were the first we had found fit to eat. Evening was drawing on, and there was nothing particularly noticeable in the half light, excepting that we crossed the Tosa, where a bridge had been broken down, and a rather curious floating substitute, on the principle of the Rhine bridges of boats, was used in its stead. Feriolo is only two or three miles from Baveno, and was preferred by us, because we knew it would be quieter and less frequented than the latter. A capital dinner and good rooms were provided by a most civil landlord, who, though master of a large house, appeared to unite in himself the situations of host, waiter, porter, and boots, and fulfilled the duties of all with equal celerity and good nature.

CHAP. IX.

Arona. — The Isola Bella. — Lago d'Orta. — Pella to Varallo. — A Pilgrimage to the Monte Sacro. — A Village Theatre. — Val Sesia. — Pass of the Val Dobbia. — Gressonay. — The Lys Glacier and Col d'Ollen. — Brusson. — Grapes and Walnuts. — Chatillon. — Aosta.

The next day was Sunday, and, wishing to see what we could of Lago Maggiore in a short time, we took the early steamboat down the lake to Arona, calling at Baveno, the Isola Bella, and several villages on the western side. The weather was not fine enough to enable us to judge fairly of this far-famed lake, and, on the whole, we were inclined to be a little disappointed. The mountain outlines around the lake seemed scarcely grand enough to be in proper proportion to the extent of water, and only in the direction of Palanza and Laveno did they at all come up to my expectations. At Arona we were once more reminded of the triumphs of man, by the unromantic presence of a railway station, where the hissing engine was offering to transport us to Turin. As, however, we had no need of its services, we spent the interval, till the time of the steamer's return, in a lounge through the somewhat dirty and very narrow principal street of the town, the chief articles of sale being grapes and figs, which we patronised pretty freely.

The return boat was full of foreigners, most of whom seemed, by their want of luggage, to be residents in the neighbourhood, and were deposited at the various pretty villages and charming villas which line the shore of the lake. The only Englishman on board was a Riffelberg acquaintance, who was going to Magadino on his way northwards. We formed a portion of a large party who landed in boats at the Isola Bella, intending to see the palace of the Borromean counts and its renowned gardens. Unfortunately the rain had, by this time, begun to fall heavily, and we resolved to wait a little for the chance of its cessation. There was, however, no improvement, so we sallied forth, and were duly lionised through the suite of public apartments: a great number of pictures, most of them indifferent, and plenty of tawdry finery, with a few pretty statues, formed the chief portion of the sight, which was hardly so interesting as Hampton

Court; and we were not sorry to find ourselves consigned to the care of a young gardener, who provided umbrellas, and prepared to show us the grounds. Here the genial nature of the climate was proved by immense red and white oleanders in sheets of blossom, and magnificent magnolias of several kinds flourishing in the highest beauty, varied with orange and citron trees in great perfection; but the construction of the terraces, raised one upon another, and ornamented with urns and statues as thickly as a stonemason's yard in the New Road, was far from pleasing to our taste, and reminded me strongly of the Perigord pie, or other marvel of the confectioner's art, to which some profane traveller has ventured to compare it.

Perhaps, if the rain had not damped the keenness of our enthusiam, we might have been in a better frame of mind for appreciating the Isola Bella; as it was, we betook ourselves to a boat without much regret, and, huddling under the awning, were rowed, or rather pushed, by two fraudulent Charons, back again to Feriolo. The clouds grew blacker than ever, and our only hope was they might weep themselves dry in the course of the night, and give us a fine day for the Lago d'Orta.

In this at least we were not disappointed: but

though the morning was exquisitely beautiful, our host declared that the heavy rain would make the road over the Monte Motterone impassable; and though we strongly suspected that this was a scheme for inducing us to take a carriage which would otherwise spend an idle day in the yard, we yielded to his opinion, and took the carriage for a drive as far as Orta. On parting he presented us with a bundle of verbenas and magnolias in full flower, and we began a most charming ride. Refreshed by the rain, nothing could be more beautiful than the luxuriance of trees, grass, and maize, with rich green orchards covered with the vines which trail from branch to branch in long festoons.

At Omegna the road approaches the side of the lake, close to which it runs as far as Orta, where we arrived in two hours from Feriolo. About a couple of miles from the town we were boarded by two stout fellows, who insisted on hanging to the back of the carriage, evidently with ulterior intentions. As we entered the charming little town, its picturesque appearance was greatly increased by a procession of ecclesiastics, chanting some service of the Church, and followed by a long train of people, who appeared to be greatly disturbed in their devotions by the necessity of staring at our party. On descending from the carriage we found our two dependents busy in unfastening the baggage, and fully prepared to take possession of us and our effects, apparently explaining in Italian, which none of us understood, that they were ready to convey us across the lake in a boat which was moored close by. In a moment a violent quarrel arose between them and the keeper of the hotel by the waterside, who evidently expected us to take his boat; but, upon the principle of "first come first served," we agreed to go with the former applicants, after stipulating with our fingers to pay only a certain number of francs.

We rowed close by the lovely island of St. Giulio, the white shining buildings upon which contrasted charmingly with the deep blue water of the lake and the thick masses of wood in front of us, through which we knew our path lay to Varallo. Upon landing at Pella, a very poor little village, we found that our two boatmen were quite prepared to be Jacks of all trades, and proposed to carry the luggage of the Prussian and our knapsacks, across the hills to Varallo, for a consideration which we did not think at all excessive: we consented, and set out at once. The path was a constant though gradual ascent, and after passing a small village called Arola, we soon found ourselves in a scene of steadily increasing beauty. Large undulating hills, rather than mountains, were around and in front of us, covered with every variety of wood, among which however the chestnut was most prominent. Every turn in the winding path revealed some new beauty, until at last we reached the highest point of the Col, and halted for a short time to enjoy the enchanting prospect.

Nothing could exceed the fresh verdure of land and wood around us: magnificent chestnuts planted by the hand of Nature overhung the path, the banks of which were covered with ferns and mountain pinks, while through the gaps among the branches we could see far over the neighbouring hills the snowy tops of some of the Monte Rosa group. The Lago d'Orta, almost at out feet, reposing in the glorious sunshine, reflected the deep blue of the cloudless sky above; and far away beyond it lay the vast plains of Sardinia, fading at last into a glowing haze, and dotted with shining white villages. It was the festival of the Nativity of the Virgin, and many a group of gaily dressed country people passed us on their return from Varallo, where they had been paying their devotions on the Monte Sacro. We turned away reluctantly from the old mossy bank, from which we had been admiring this Paradise of scenery, and began to descend by a path of equal beauty with that which we had ascended from Pella. On the way down we discovered a great quantity of the sweet-scented cyclamen, as delicately sweet as the lily of the valley; and presently found ourselves on the high road from Arona and central Piedmont, which continued to wind among green valleys and richly wooded hills, generally conical in form, until, in about three hours from Pella, we arrived at Varallo.

All was gaiety and activity, in consequence of the numbers of people drawn by the occasion of the fête to the venerated Monte Sacro. Finding that we should have time enough before dinner, we determined to make the pilgrimage to the Sacred Mount at once, and as it completely overlooks the town, there was no difficulty in finding the right way. Turning out of the main street to the right, a sloping paved way leads up the side of the hill, very much like that which approaches the castle of Heidelberg. Two or three chapels with life-size figures in them ornamented the way, and about half way up, a large wooden cross stood by the side of the path, surrounded by four or five old women reciting Paters and Aves, and whittling chips from it with a zeal that might astonish the most energetic Yankee. A few zigzags under the trees brought us to a small *café* for the restoration of exhausted pilgrims, close to which a doorway led into the sacred enclosure. The pilgrimage consists in visiting forty or fifty shrines or chapels, barred in front like the cages in the Zoological Gardens, and containing groups of figures illustrating Scriptural subjects from the Creation to the Resurrection in regular order. The figures are many of them done exceedingly well, though the grotesque element has been rather too largely admitted: Herod's servants, for instance, are sometimes represented with most disgusting goîtres; and in one case the artist has ornamented that monarch's court with a very comical mediæval dwarf, holding a dog as tall as himself, and looking at the soldiers with an expression of the most mischievous drollery.

All the chapels are numbered, and arranged in such an order, that the visitor who follows the path has to pass backwards and forwards an infinity of times before he can complete his pilgrimage. Money is thrown in through the gratings; and as this was an especial occasion, some of the more favourite shrines had their floor completely covered with the offerings of the faithful, which are, I suppose, collected by the priests at the end of their day's work. Altogether, the Monte Sacro is a very curious place, and well worthy of a visit, even if the surrounding scenery were not so exquisitely lovely.

Hearing there was a theatre in the town, we went to look for it after dinner, and on payment of eight sous were admitted into a long room, with the seats all level, on the stage at the end of which was being performed a melodrama very much in the style of Richardson's, except as to the length of the performance; for after seeing it, I think, into the fifth act, with no prospect of a termination, as the hero appeared to be still overwhelmed with most grievous difficulties, we retired to the hotel and went to bed.

The next day we were to ascend the Val Sesia to Riva or Alagna, and, finding there was a car-road as far as Scopello, we engaged a small vehicle to convey two of the party with the baggage to that place. The other two walked; and, as the road was sometimes rough, we found we were not much beaten by the carriage. At Scopello we engaged two strapping women to take our effects up to Riva, and, sending them on ahead, we entered a small wineshop for luncheon. This place consisted of one room, about eight feet square, ornamented with highly imaginative pictures of the battles of 1848, and patriotic declarations in favour of the late king Carlo Alberto, and was otherwise filled with pickles, wine-flasks, lemonade, candles, grocery, and smoke, the latter of which poured through the door from an adjoining apartment in such volumes that we were obliged to take our refreshment *al fresco* on a bench outside.

We then continued our walk up as lovely a valley as could well be imagined, with birch-trees waving over the banks of the foaming river, followed by ash, chestnut, and pine, soaring one over the other to the very tops of the hills on either side of it. Campertogno and Mollia especially were most enchanting spots, and then a turn of the path to the right suddenly showed us the head of the valley, with Monte Rosa looking down upon us from its extremity, all glistening in the deep blue sky. Early in the afternoon we arrived at Riva, a miserable village, where however we resolved to sleep, with the view of crossing the Val Dobbia to Gressonay on the next day. The little inn was the worst we stayed at in the course of the journey, and there would have been some difficulty in getting anything to eat, had it not been for the very fortunate circumstance, that the various ecclesiastics of the valley meditated a dinner there on the following day, and we were enabled to taste the first-fruits of an extra importation of provisions. The fare, however, was very rough, and two of our party were quite unable to taste what the good woman seemed to think was a particular luxury in the way of soup, served up in large coffee-cups. A hanger-on in the house was very anxious to inform us that he had served in the Crimea with the Sardinian army, and had obtained the English medal; but as he did not offer to produce it, and was not a particularly honest-looking fellow, we did not feel quite satisfied of his veracity.

We started early in the morning, and crossed the Val Dobbia to Gressonay. This pass is certainly the most uninteresting I have seen, and I should strongly advise everyone to go to Alagna instead of stopping at Riva, and thence cross to Gressonay by the Col d'Ollen, which, though somewhat more fatiguing, is infinitely more worth seeing, passing, as it does, close to the foot of Monte Rosa and the Lyskamm. At the highest point of the Val Dobbia is a miserable little building, dignified by the name of Hospice, where, however, we got some tolerable bread and cheese. Just in front, at a distance of about four miles, was an opening in the chain of mountains which form the western boundary of the valley below us; and this we could easily see must be the Col de Ranzola, over which we were to pass to Brusson and Chatillon.

The evening was dull and cold, as we entered Gressonay, and we were very glad to huddle round a handsome wood-fire after dinner in the clean and comfortable *salle à manger*. There were only two other strangers in the house, a gentleman and lady, who turned out to be no strangers to one of us, and helped us to pass a very pleasant evening. A lame foot owned by one of the party prevented him from marching far on the following day, and it was accordingly resolved to stay all together at Gressonay, and explore the head of the valley and the glacier from the Lyskamm.

After breakfast I started with my new friend, Mr. S., and a guide whom he had brought with him, and in about an hour arrived at Trinita, soon after passing which we had a good view of the Lyskamm and its glacier. The weather was, unfortunately, far from settled, and the great problem of the day was, whether the morning clouds would disperse or come down upon us with a shift of wind to the westward, of which there were indications on the further hills: the solution of our doubt was at hand, and presently a great dark mass of clouds came rolling down from the west with a rain that made waterproofs necessary till we found some shelter. As the storm passed, the dark mountains on each side of the valley showed their heads again, thoroughly whitened by the snow just fallen upon them, and for a moment we hoped for an improvement in the weather; but the clouds returned to the charge, and the head of the valley was so entirely enveloped in them, that it became perfectly useless to attempt a nearer approach to the glacier. On our way back we turned into the little church of Trinita to avoid another pelting shower, and the curé, who was passing, begged us most good-naturedly to come with him into his house close by. We accepted the offer with gratitude, and were admitted by him into a small but neat house, in which, however, he seemed only to occupy one room, with, I suppose, the use of a kitchen. His room was plain and simple in the extreme, with a common truckle-bed at one side of it, and a small table at the other which, with some drawers, and a few common chairs and old-fashioned ornaments, seemed to complete his furniture. His little library consisted of only about twenty books, some of which, however, he showed us with peculiar pleasure as remembrances of his old student days in Germany, where he had been educated. A most kind man he evidently was, and talked with great interest of his parishioners, who are a superior race to the natives of all the neighbouring valleys; they are of German origin, and preserve their German language and manners quite distinct from the corruptions of their neighbours. The curé wanted to bring wine for us, but not wishing to trespass upon his hospitality, we told him that we had taken some provisions up the valley with us in the morning; and after half an hour's agreeable conversation, we left him, and returned to the inn at Gressonay.

We all dined very pleasantly together, and late in the evening the party was increased by the arrival of two young Englishmen, who had come over from Brusson in a soaking rain, and were not a little pleased to find themselves at our comfortable fireside. They were pressed for time, and, in spite of the wretched weather, were determined to get to Alagna by the Col d'Ollen next day, and as our party were equally resolved to wait for more favouring skies, I promised to spend the day in accompanying them to the top of the Col and returning to Gressonay.

They took a guide, and a mule for their baggage, and directly after breakfast we started in full reliance on our waterproof coats, though rain was evidently to be the order of the day. I learnt from them the first news of what has produced such a profound sensation in England—the failure of the Royal British Bank. After passing Trinita once more, and the next village of St. Giacomo, we turned to the right, and began the ascent towards the Col d'Ollen, every step bringing us into a more cold and disagreeable rain and sleet; but as it is never certain that noon may not bring a change for the better in mountain districts, and as I would rather do anything than pass an idle day, I still kept to my resolution, and walked while my two companions took turns upon the mule. Now and then, through the clouds, we had some splendid peeps of the Lyskamm—just enough to satisfy me that this pass must be an exceedingly fine one in good weather; but as the way was very wild, without any defined path in its upper regions, I had to make the observation of neighbouring landmarks my principal object, knowing that I should have to return alone, and that on a very bad day. This becoming more and more and more difficult, I at last made up my mind to turn back about half an hour before reaching the highest point of the Col, and accordingly said farewell to my companions. I found that I had noted my way correctly, and had no difficulty in finding the track to St. Giacomo, whence there is a good mule-road to Gressonay. On my way back, I was rewarded for a supererogatory scramble up the rocks on the left, by finding a few Alpine rhododendrons still in bloom, long after they had ceased flowering almost everywhere else. On rejoining the party at the inn, I found that they had dragged a monstrous log of fir up to the house, which kept up a blaze all the evening.

Next morning matters mended, and leaving our friends, Mr. S. and his wife, to go over to Alagna, we prepared to move in the other direction towards Chatillon in the Val d'Aosta. A porter was sent for to carry the knapsacks in one of the customary wicker-frames, but I was surprised to find him too lazy to carry more than one of them. I shut the door in his face, telling him I would send for a woman to do the work; even this taunt, however, had not the slightest effect, and ultimately a boy was found who eagerly volunteered to carry two of them. About an hour and a half brought us to the summit of the Col de Ranzola, which commands a very fine view of the Lyskamm and part of the Monte Rosa group in one direction, and the long line of the Val d'Aosta in the other. The city itself was distinctly visible, but Mont Blanc, being rather too much to the right, is hidden by an intervening mountain. After about an hour's descent over rough ground and scanty pastures, a sudden turn in the road discovered Brusson at our feet and a great part of the valley which leads up to St. Giacomo d'Ayas, and the foot of our old friend the Breithorn. Brusson is a filthy village containing, however, one house, which belongs to the curé, equal in size and value to nearly all the others put together. Whilst we were talking to him, some miserable-looking crétins came up to beg, and he told us that there was a sadly large number of them in the neighbourhood: poor harmless wretches! they are incapable of steady work, and are entirely dependent upon national and individual charity. The little inn was difficult to find, and very rough and homely: the host, however, appeared to have some pride of birth, and had hung the walls of a miserable room with most grotesque portraits of various members of his family; such, at least, I suppose they were.

From Brusson the path again ascends through a fine fir wood, with good turf to walk on over the upper part of an inconsiderable col, and then descends to St. Vincent, the latter part of the way lying amongst magnificent walnut and chestnut trees, completely covered with fruit. All the richness of the Val d'Aosta was now before us: Chatillon, at about two miles' distance, shone with its white buildings among masses of wood; and St. Vincent, close to us, and surrounded with pretty villas and beautifully kept vineyards, loaded with magnificent black grapes, showed signs of a prosperity that we had not seen for several days. We reached Chatillon in about seven hours from Gressonay, and in the new hotel, close to the noisy little river which comes down the Val Tournanche from the snows of the Matterhorn, we feasted on grapes and peaches while a car was being prepared to take us to Aosta. The growth of maize and vines throughout this valley is very luxuriant, but many parts of it evidently suffer from the furious torrents which in spring and wet weather rush down from the mountains to join the Dora Baltea, which was even now boiling along in large stormy waves. The great blight of the valley is the enormous amount of goîtres and crétinism, which make the inhabitants a perfectly hideous race. As we entered the village of Nuz, out of the first seven persons I saw, six were more or less palpably crétins. Those who are afflicted with this most dreadful plague have generally short shambling figures, with unnaturally large round heads, the faces of which have no expression but a horrid leer; in addition to which their disgusting habits constitute them the very lowest order of the human race, scarcely, if any, better than the beasts that perish.

A three hours' drive from Chatillon brought us to the Écu at Aosta, and after strolling out to look at the Roman arches, which are built of large blocks of shingly stones cemented together like concrete, we made ourselves comfortable for the evening.

CHAP. X.

Stormy Weather on the St. Bernard. — Col Fenêtre and Col Ferrex. — Courmayeur. — The Proments. — Col de Checruit. — Col de la Seigne. — Col des Fours. — A Party lost. — Contamines. — Col de Voza. — The new Route to the Summit of Mont Blanc. — Les Ouches. — Chamonix.

THE Cité d'Aoste, in spite of its ambitious title, is but a very poor place in modern times, though the extent of its Roman remains may indicate that it was formerly considered of greater importance. A dirty street, scarcely so wide as a large omnibus, without any protection for foot passengers, leads into the only open space in the town, which is a tolerably large square, containing two or three hotels and some government buildings, with a market occupying the largest part of the centre. There appeared, however, to be nothing for sale in the whole town but articles of the commonest description. Like the inhabitants of all the rest of the valley, the citizens of Aosta seemed, for the most part, rather a miserable race, though some pretty houses spread about the outskirts indicated the presence of a superior class. The Hôtel de la Poste is abominably dirty, and the Écu not much better, though the people of the house were very civil and obliging. Since leaving the country last September, I have heard from Jean Tairraz, of Chamonix, who has just opened a new hotel at Aosta, called the Hôtel du Mont Blanc, in hopes of making a residence there more palatable to the cleanly English than it can be at present. He has been several times as a chief guide to the summit of Mont Blanc; and I have found, from many a day's experience of him, with various kinds of parties, that he knows how to combine the boldness of a good glacier guide with all the delicacy and care which ladies can so fully appreciate on the Mer de Glace or the Mauvais Pas; and having lived much with English families, he is sure to do his utmost towards retrieving the dirty character of Aosta.

About nightfall heavy clouds again threatened unpleasantly about the mountains, and in the morning all the neighbouring heights being powdered with snow, testified to the coldness which we might expect to find at the Grand St. Bernard. In spite, however, of a pamphlet inviting travellers to pass a fortnight at Aosta, and professing to find a new lion for every day, we made up our minds to go on to the Hospice, in the hope of getting good weather for the tour of Mont Blanc. We started soon after breakfast, with rather a fine morning in the valley, but an ominous gathering of clouds on the mountains before us.

The road leaving the city runs northward under an avenue of walnuts, which supplied us with light provisions for the march, and presently turning to the right it ascends slowly, but steadily, through a fine district of vineyards. Placed thus advantageously on the slopes facing the south, the vines attain a very great luxuriance, and the grapes, though not quite ripe, hung in a profusion and beauty which would almost have done credit to our finest hot-houses. But the level of vineyards was soon passed, and was succeeded by plenty of walnut and chestnut trees, loaded with fruit, and growing out of charmingly green meadows ornamented with the lilac flowers of the autumn crocus. As we passed the village of Gignaud, the bells of the church began to ring in a fashion which I think is peculiar to Piedmont. Commencing slowly and regularly, they suddenly burst out into a kind of rollicking jig, the tune of which occasionally changed, although the style continued without much variety. This lively melody seemed intended to prepare the mind for the expected jollity of "the Monks of Old" at the top of the pass; and we hoped that it might be a good omen.

At this point of the route there is a fine view of the Valpellina to the right, leading up to Prarayen, and the still imperfectly known regions between the St. Bernard and the Zermatt mountains. In about four hours from Aosta we arrived at St. Remy, a small village perched in a narrow cleft between mountains which seem almost ready to suffocate it, but which no doubt afford a friendly shelter in the severe weather which prevails here during the greater part of the year. This is the nearest place to the frontier, and accordingly a party of *douaniers* is placed here to examine passports; this solemn farce was soon performed, and, bidding adieu to car roads for some days to come, we started up the mule-path towards the famous Hospice.

Before long we found ourselves fairly among the clouds which had been hanging over our heads, and the light driving rain was rather agreeably exchanged for a snowstorm. By the time we reached the level of the house of refuge, the ground was thickly covered with snow, and there was every probability of our reaching the monks in a very appropriate state of discomfort. As we climbed up the last slope, a lift in the clouds showed us over our heads the cross which is fixed in the rocks to point out the top of the pass. Leaving this on the left, the path is cut through a narrow gorge, or funnel, for a short distance, through which the wind beat so violently that it was scarcely possible to keep one's breath and fight through; the rocks on each side had been covered with half-melted snow, which formed into rows of long icicles, not hanging straight down, but forced into a slanting direction by the tremendous fury of the gale. Within a yard of our feet was the tarn, or mountain lake, its waters dashing in angry waves upon the bank; but the storm-fog was so dense that we could not see a dozen yards across it. Had I not known the way, I should have almost despaired of reaching the Hospice; but a struggle of ten minutes brought us to a huge shade in the mist, and we found ourselves suddenly within ten paces of its walls, till then entirely invisible. Drifted snow was piled around the door-steps, and nothing short of being dragged in on the dogs' backs could have been more in accordance with the genius of the place than our entrance into this world-renowned refuge for the destitute and way-worn traveller.

Once inside, and the howling tempest is exchanged for a scene of perfect comfort and tranquillity: the huge thick walls are utterly regardless of the storm, and the moment the bell is rung, the polite and gentlemanly *clavendier* receives you with all the charm of a host who wishes to make his guests perfectly comfortable; he shows you into a bedroom far better than almost any to be found in continental hotels, insists on sending up plenty of hot brandy-and-water, and leaves you to make your toilet in a most enviable frame of mind.

When this was completed, we descended and found him ready to welcome us to the cheerful fire, blazing with logs, which are all brought on the backs of mules from the convent forest, several leagues distant. Nearly a dozen travellers were collected in the room, several of whom had been detained since the day before by the tempestuous state of the weather; and among them was a very agreeable young American, the only man of his nation whom I have ever found really enjoying walking among the mountains. He was very different from one of his countrymen, whose entry I saw in a " Livre des Étrangers: " — " Thank God, we don't raise such hills in the state of New York!"

In 1855, I met at the Hospice a dentist, who

spoke French with a fine nasal Yankee twang, which by no means improved that refined and most elegant language. He employed his leisure time in filling up little blue tickets with the name and address of his firm in Paris and New York, which I found he was in the habit of sticking on walls and window-sills in the hotels where he lodged, in imitation of the "elegies upon hawthorns," which Orlando dedicated to the beauty of the fair Rosalind. He was altogether a sharp practitioner, and I should hardly have been surprised at hearing that he had offered to pull out the monks' teeth, instead of rewarding their hospitality in the more customary manner.

A capital dinner was served, the cooking of which would have done credit to many a fine house in the valleys, with plenty of excellent wine, which is said to be the offering of the King of Sardinia. The *clavendier*, after taking care that the ladies had the best places, seated himself at the table, and contrived, with all the ease and native elegance of a man of the world, to bring every member of the party into conversation upon some one or other of the topics of the day, mixed with much interesting information relating to the affairs of the hospice, in which he has resided eleven years.

After dinner he showed us the curiosities of the

little museum, which contains a variety of prints, presented by people from all parts of the world, and a very pretty collection of Roman bronze statuettes and ornaments, which have been from time to time dug up in the neighbourhood of the Hospice walls, to bear testimony of the ubiquity of that wonderful people. The severity of the climate here is so great that the snow never leaves the ground for nine months in the year; and many of the monks suffer very severely, but he himself seemed as fresh as if he had only been subjected to the ordinary lot of man.

Next morning the frost was severe, and the fog still continued so thick, that we were advised to wait another day; but on consulting the barometer, and finding it on the rise, our kind host said that we might venture to proceed, and went to find us what we wanted — a guide across the mountains to Courmayeur. He found a man below who offered to take us; but it soon appeared that he wanted to go by the comparatively tame Serena pass, whilst I was resolved upon the Col Fenêtre. He tried to persuade me that the latter would be an affair of at least twelve hours, but fortunately I knew better, having crossed the pass only a year before; and, after a little battling, all was arranged for an immediate start. We paid an early visit to the interesting chapel, and deposited our offering in the " Tronc des aumônes; " were introduced to the dogs, unhappily almost extinct; peeped into the ghastly morgue, where the bones of lost travellers are whitening in an air whose purity seems to defy putrefaction, and then departed, after a cordial farewell from our kind entertainer.

The route from the St. Bernard by the Col Fenêtre seems much less known than it deserves to be, for it presents a great variety of scenery, and forms a very capital introduction to the tour of Mont Blanc. On leaving the Hospice we retraced our steps of yesterday by the side of the lake, and for some little distance down below the cross. There we turned to the right, and began a considerable ascent over the rocks by a path which was now entirely covered with snow; so that though I had crossed it previously, and knew the general line pretty well, I should have had some difficulty in acting as sole guide, surrounded as we still were by a fog of very uncomfortable density. We often had to wade through snow far above our knees, which was sometimes driven in whirlwinds by the fierce gale, that became a perfect hurricane when, after climbing up a very steep slope, we found ourselves on the top of the Col, about 1000 feet above the Hospice. None of the party wished to stay long in such an exposed situation, and quickly plunging with long strides down through the deep drifts of snow, we soon found ourselves close to some small tarns which occupy the base of a kind of crater among the mountains that raise their ragged peaks around.

We next began to descend upon the upper pastures, and heard the tinkle of cattle-bells sounding close to us, though the mist prevented us from seeing their bearers; but in a few minutes more we had descended through the cloud, and came suddenly into a fine sunny day, with the long line of valley spread out before us in all its beauty, and terminated by the northern spurs of the Mont Blanc group. Such a wonderful transition could not fail to raise our spirits, and, rapidly descending across the pastures, we soon arrived at the bottom of the gorge, and crossed the stream which traverses it by an overarching bridge of snow. Hence the ascent towards the south is rather long and monotonous; and being now covered with quantities of fresh snow, half melted by the sun, the grassy ground was difficult to walk upon. We arrived, however, at the top of the Col Ferrex in about four hours from the Hospice, and were immediately face to face with all the glories of Mont Blanc, and the long line of Aiguilles and glaciers, reaching as far as the Col de la Seigne. Such a sight would compensate for much more serious inconvenience than we had sustained in the morning. A descent of half an hour brought us to the châlets of Pré de Bar, close to the foot of the Glacier de Triolet, which once discharged an immense mass of ice into the valley, destroying everything before it. This glacier, and the next in order, which comes down from the Grande Jorasse, bring with them frequent remains of the now almost extinct *bouquetin* or *steinbok*, showing that this part of the mountains must have been one of their most favourite haunts. They are very rarely seen in the Alps now, and Lochmatter despaired of them; but a short time before we arrived in the neighbourhood, a magnificent specimen, with rings upon his horns marking thirty years of age, was shot by a Courmayeur man on one of the Jorasses, and my guide carried the head and horns to Chamonix, where he said he sold them for 120 francs. Lochmatter would, I believe, have gone wild, if he could have known it.

We walked rapidly down the valley, amid the

most magnificent scenery, and arrived at Courmayeur early in the afternoon, after a walk of about eight hours, in all, from the St. Bernard. At the door of the hotel I found my old friend, the ex-Sergeant-major Proment, an excellent fellow who served in the wars of Napoleon, and then settled down among his mountains, where he was for many years well known as the chief guide in the place. Getting too old for this work, he has resigned in favour of his nephews, and contents himself with showing a book of his certificates for the last thirty years, and talking over old adventures.

If I were asked in what place I had seen sublimity and beauty of scenery combined more than anywhere else, I should undoubtedly give the palm to Courmayeur and its immediate environs. The views from the green meadows of Pré St. Didier, and throughout the short distance between the two villages, are wonderfully fine. The exquisite freshness of the grass, the variety of wood, the overhanging precipices of the Cramont, and the lofty summit of the Mont Chétif, leading the eye up to the gigantic Jorasses, the Dent du Géant, and the snowy summit of Mont Blanc, 12,000 feet above the valley, form a spectacle which can never be forgotten by those who have once seen it. Probably the view of Monte Rosa and the Macugnaga glacier from the Val Anzasca, may be a worthy rival, but the state of the weather when we were there permitted us to see nothing but clouds.

The Cramont ought to be ascended from Courmayeur, but in 1855 we had no weather fine enough for it, and in 1856 no time. The best substitute is to take the route of the Col de Checruit, and so get to the Col de la Seigne, instead of keeping the line of the Allée Blanche by the glaciers of Brenva and Miage. This pass appears to be scarcely known, and its existence is only casually alluded to by Professor Forbes. I think, therefore, that, considering its beauty, I may be doing a service in recommending it to the attention of travellers, though, to those who wish to examine the glaciers accurately, it would be advisable to spend a day previously in an expedition to the Brenva and Miage.

We crossed the river immediately opposite to Courmayeur, instead of following it up the valley, and passing through the village of Dolina, at once commenced ascending through a charming piece of country, ending in a long grassy slope at the back of the Mont Chétif; and in about an hour and a half we found ourselves at a great height in the upper part of a splendid pine-forest, exactly opposite the precipitous side of Mont Blanc. The wonderful beauty of this view is enhanced by its breaking upon one suddenly: in a moment the whole chain, as far as the Col Ferrex, hitherto concealed by the intervening height, bursts upon the eye; whereas the route of the Allée Blanche lies so completely under the great chain, that very little can be seen of it. Here precipice on precipice, aiguille on aiguille, is seen reaching from the valley to the very summit, 12,000 feet above; and the forest-clad side of the singular Mont Chétif forms no inconsiderable feature in the spectacle. The immense Aiguille of the Peteret, flanked by two exactly similar rocky points of smaller size, forms, as it were, the back and sides of a huge Gothic chair, the intermediate space, corresponding to the seat, being a patch of green pasture at a great height above the valley, and only approached by climbing up apparently inaccessible precipices. Proment, however, assured me, that this scrap of vegetation is not lost sight of by the prudent inhabitants of Courmayeur; and as soon as the winter snows disappear, about the end of June, thirty or forty sheep are carried up, one by one, on men's backs, and left there without any possibility of getting away from their prison. At the end of the three months' summer, they are brought down again; and, though it is generally found that three or four of them have been killed, by falling ice or rocks, the remainder are so fat, and in such capital condition, that the speculation completely answers.

Turning sharply to the left, the way to be taken steadily ascends considerably above the level of the highest woods, till Mont Chétif itself is seen below, instead of towering above; and then a rapid descent over pastures leads down to some rude châlets a little above the Combal lake. At these châlets I observed two rough but very useful instruments: one was a long nail hammered into the centre of a board which was marked with figures and hung on a wall facing the south, to do the duty of a sun-dial worthy of Robinson Crusoe: the other was a small water-wheel, about four feet in diameter, turned by a noisy little mountain stream; to the end of its axle was attached a tub, which of course turned with it, and being filled with cream, and left to itself, could churn butter without the aid of manual labour.

A little lower down we came to the dreary lake, which is formed by the damming up of the water by the vast moraine of the Glacier de Miage, that fills up the valley with the exception of one narrow outlet and extends downwards for several miles. In addition to the magnificent view obtained from the Col de Checruit, a great advantage is gained by pursuing that route, in avoiding the rough disagreeable walk over this immense pile of rocky *detritus*, all of which Professor Forbes discovered was brought down from a vast gorge in the very heart of Mont Blanc. Near the lake a pure spring, that mingles its clear waters with the turbid meltings of the glaciers, is well worthy of being tasted. From this point a somewhat dreary ascent of rather more than an hour and a half leads to the top of the Col de la Seigne; and this reminds me of a story of two Frenchmen.

In 1855 two young Parisian *avocats*, who were with us at the St. Bernard, expressed a wish to travel in our company to Chamonix. We started together for the Col Fenêtre, but before the day was half over, one of them took to hanging behind, and gave us some annoyance in waiting for him: upon this, a violent quarrel ensued between the two, who had been travelling as the dearest friends for the last six weeks: they ended by calling each other "Monsieur," and, dividing their travelling-stores, parted as if never more to meet, one going on with us to Courmayeur, while the other was left behind to follow his own devices. Our companion was exceedingly sociable, but on arriving at Courmayeur he refused to give half a franc more than he thought proper for his bed, and parted with us to go to the other hotel, with the understanding that we should meet in the morning. His quondam friend must have joined him there in the course of the evening, and next day we found they had started together early, though by no means reconciled as it would seem; for on mentioning the story a few days afterwards, at Chamonix, I found that they had been seen sitting on the top of the Col de la Seigne, eating their luncheon *dos à dos*, and evidently determined not to speak to one another. So much for friendship!

On the top of the Col we found a very severe wind, and, looking up to the white summit of Mont Blanc, we could see a smoke-like film of powdery snow driven by the gale, which showed how hard a matter it would have been to live there that day. The Tarentaise was before us to the south-west, and we were not very long in descending several thousand feet to Mottet, where we soon ensconced ourselves in the smallest edifice that ever claimed the title of an inn. In the two previous years I had gone on to Chapiu, and crossed the Col du Bonhomme; but having, on one occasion, been kept awake the whole night by a gang of drunken cattle-drivers returning from a fair at St. Maurice, and, on the other, by a horde of not less troublesome fleas, I resolved this time to try Mottet and the Col des Fours.

In the morning we started with cloudless weather, and after a very steep climb reached the summit of the Col, which we found covered with deep fresh snow, noticing by the way some coffin-like wooden devices on short legs, in which the luckless shepherds shut themselves up for the night during the few months when their charges are on the high pastures. With regard to cattle, I found that the great Sardinian owners let their beasts to the mountaineers at the rate of fifteen or eighteen francs apiece for the three summer months, during which the lessees make all they can of them in the way of cheese and butter, and then they are driven down again to the more temperate plains. In 1855 we saw a large covey of birds near the top of the Col, which we knew to be ptarmigan, in spite of our guide's assertion that they were "pigeons sauvages;" and a capital day's sport we might have had if we had been provided with guns.

On the northern side of the Col we found a party of men employed in improving the path, and not before it was needed, as was testified by the clean-picked skeleton of a mule which had fallen over early in the spring with the man who accompanied it; both were killed, but the man had been taken away and buried, while the poor beast was left to the tender mercies of eagles and tornadoes. This pass has been marked by disasters: a little lower down is the spot where two Englishmen perished some years back in a snow-storm; they had two friends with them, and the guides endeavoured to urge them on, not hesitating even to use their *bâtons*, till, finding death must be the lot of the whole party if they waited longer, they were compelled to leave them to their fate. At Nantbourant we saw their last hand-writing, in which they noted their departure for the Col, seemingly in the highest spirits. Before reaching the forest below, there is another sad memorial, in the shape of a cairn of stones on a place called the Plan des Dames, where there is a legend of a lady and her maid having long ago perished, and every traveller pays a tribute to their memory by adding a fresh stone to the pile.

Passing among magnificent pines, we reached the litte hamlet of Nantbourant, beyond which the path, ever increasing in beauty, leaves the chapel and shrines of Notre Dame de la Gorge on the left, and in another hour leads to Contamines. Here we slept at the little Hôtel du Bonhomme, rendered memorable on a previous visit by a great sensation caused by a party of two Frenchmen and three ladies, whose mules arrived at midnight, the travellers having been lost on the Col du Bonhomme, where they allowed their mules to go on alone, whilst they walked down under the escort of a bad guide, who, in the darkness of the evening, led them by mistake into the Val de Beaufort; where, after wandering about till their shoes were torn off, they were all obliged to sleep as best they could in a hay châlet till the mules returned for them with their luggage in the morning.

Next day a pleasant walk took us in about three hours to the pavilion on the Col de Voza, overlooking the Glacier de Bionnassay, from which the St. Gervais ascent of Mont Blanc was made in 1855, and recorded in the interesting account of Messrs. Hudson and Kennedy. The Chamonix men quaked in their shoes at the tidings of this new and cheap route being discovered; but their spirits have somewhat recovered their equilibrium on finding that all the attempts to follow the new path in 1856 have, from various circumstances, failed. It is, no doubt, a good and practicable way; but the unpleasantness of sleeping on the Aiguille du Gouté seems a considerable obstacle, and those who have tried it, report that the danger of stones continually falling from the Aiguille is not to be disregarded.

After enjoying the lovely view of the valley of Chamonix from this Col, which commands not only the Mont Blanc chain, but a vast array of the mountains on the other side of the valley, we descended to Les Ouches, and, passing by the pure beauty of the Glacier des Bossons, arrived at the Hôtel de Londres at Chamonix soon after mid-day.

CHAP. XI.

The Mer de Glace. — Expedition to the Jardin. — Chamonix Guides. — The Glacier de Taléfre. — The Brevent. — Jean Tairraz. — The Pierre de l'Échelle. — Excursion to the Glaciers at the Foot of the Aiguilles. — A Discovery. — Return to Chamonix.

WE had now enjoyed four days of perfectly fine weather since leaving the St. Bernard; but, on the afternoon of reaching Chamonix, a thin white fleecy cloud settling round the upper part of Mont Blanc, and gradually extending itself in all directions, gave indications of a change. We afterwards found that one of my Monte Rosa companions was then trying to ascend the mountain from St. Gervais, having with a party of guides slept on the Aiguille du Gouté: they had reached the crest of the Dome du Gouté, when the cloud which we had seen prevented completing the ascent, and they were obliged to descend to the Grand Plateau and across the Glacier des Bossons to Chamonix. At night the whole sky was covered with clouds, and when, after a wet day and night there was a temporary clearance, it was evident that the season was over, and a premature winter had set in. No longer satisfied with the tops of the mountains, the snow had descended so low that the pine-forest between Montanvert and the valley was completely whitened, and a considerable degree of cold prevailed, even in the village. We persevered, however, in walking up to the Montanvert inn, amid heavily falling snow, and a most beautiful sight it was, to see all the magnificent trees among which we passed loaded with their white burdens. On first arriving, we could not see across the Mer de Glace, but presently the air cleared, and the magnificent Dru and Verte Aiguilles gleamed forth in a sunshine till then denied to us. The beauty of the glacier was greatly increased by six inches of fresh snow which covered it, and prevented our seeing any of the dirt which generally blots some of its purity.

After an amusing scramble over the ice, which was much easier than usual to walk upon in consequence of the snow, we returned to Chamonix, highly delighted with all the enchanting effects produced by weather so inauspicious-looking in the valley as to keep most of the visitors confined to the fireside of the hotel.

A few days later, we tried to get to the Jardin without guides, trusting to the fact of two of us having been there previously; but we started too late, and the difficulty of the way was so greatly increased by the quantities of snow, that, though I knew the route perfectly, a doubt on the part of some as to the utility of further progress when near the foot of the Egralets was followed by a return to the village. After this, matters meteorological grew decidedly worse, and we abandoned the campaign for the season, thinking ourselves fortunate in getting a day sufficiently fine to go by the Tête Noire to Martigny, whence we reached the more genial climate of the lake of Geneva on our way homewards by Berne, Basle, and the Rhine, to Rotterdam and Amsterdam.

Matters were, however, very different at the same time in the year 1855, and I prefer thinking of the successful expeditions of that season to dwelling on the failures of the last. In the September of that year, Dundas and I spent a fortnight at Chamonix, and were enabled to explore the country thoroughly, with the exception of ascending Mont Blanc, the monarch. We had the great advantage of having brought young Proment with us from Courmayeur, who knew the Chamonix neighbourhood as well as a native of the valley, and was willing to go with us anywhere, for the regular charge of six francs a day, being entirely free from the detestable regulations of Chamonix. The system of the incorporated guides is a great nuisance: everybody who wishes to make an excursion from Chamonix, whether the Montanvert or the top of Mont Blanc be the object of ambition, must take his guides according to the *rôle*, whether he is well acquainted with their reputation or an utter stranger to their name. Were they all equally excellent, this would not be a great hardship, but the contrary is the fact; and none grumble at the system so much as the really first-rate guides, of whom there are plenty at Chamonix, who find themselves put on a level with men scarcely more fit for their duties than so many railway porters.

The number made necessary by the tariff, and the rate of payment, are both absurdly exorbitant, nor can they be relaxed even in the case of all the party being as experienced as themselves upon the ice, and only wanting some one to point out the shortest way to the desired object. It would be a real pleasure to have a day's excursion with a Tairraz, a Couttet, a Simond, or a Balmat, but while the regulations prevent a choice of guides, it is well worth while to do as we did, and bring a good man from Courmayeur, to set them at defiance.

For the expedition to the Jardin, we should have been compelled to take two guides, the first on the list, and pay them ten francs apiece; and it was quite amusing to watch the faces of some of the hangers-on about the hotel, as we started with Proment alone; and not less so when we returned, after completing the excursion in an extraordinarily short time. We left the hotel about half-past seven on a beautiful morning, and got to the Montanvert in an hour and a half: here, having bought a cold chicken, some eggs, and a couple of bottles of wine, we moved pretty rapidly along the path by the side of the Mer de Glace, passed the rocks called Les Ponts, where a few steps, about an inch wide, are cut in the face of the stone, and soon after took to the glacier. On approaching the promontory of Trélaporte, the ice is so rent and torn by impassable crevasses of very great depth, that it is necessary to take once more to *terra firma*, and climb a rocky path which leads down again to the glacier nearly opposite the Egralets, in the direction of which we moved across the ice, crossing the successive moraines and jumping over the crevasses, or picking our way among their mazes when they were too formidable to be crossed in the more adventurous and active manner.

And, now, round the corner of the Egralets we

came in sight of the great broken mass of the Glacier de Taléfre. The bed of the glacier being here exceedingly steep, the whole body of ice is torn and rent into a thousand forms as it is slowly urged on its downward course: pile upon pile, terrace upon terrace, with vast blue chasms between them, stretch bristling across the sky, the whole looking as if some giant Niagara had been broken up by contact with innumerable rocks, and then frozen in an instant. Looking at it with a telescope, I could see that many of the masses were on the very point of falling, and presently a low dull roar, echoed from the precipices of the Tacul, announced that the expectant chasm had received its prey. Forbes has stated that a knapsack which was lost, in 1836, between the Jardin and this part of the glacier was found in 1846 at the foot of the Couvercle, having in the ten years moved over four thousand three hundred feet of the glacier, and descended through eleven hundred and forty-five feet of elevation.

No mortal man dare attempt to climb the ice at this part; and leaving the glacier, we ascended the Egralets by a rough and narrow path, which in due time brought us on a level with the upper ice. By the side of this path, and close to a large patch of snow, is some grass-covered ground ornamented with a few wild flowers; and a guide, in a moment of weakness, once admitted to me that this place was known to some of them as the Jardin des Dames, on account of a very excusable imposition, by which they sometimes persuade over-adventurous ladies and fatigued gentlemen, that they have seen the renowned Jardin about an hour and a half short of the reality, and thereby save them all the trouble and difficulty of crossing the upper part of the Glacier de Taléfre.

From this point the way was diversified by frequent beds of snow among the rough rocky district, and at last we found ourselves once more setting out upon the glacier, which at this part is particularly disagreeable, being intersected with rills of water in great abundance, making their way among a mixture of half-melted snow and ice, and occasionally hiding their course so completely under the surface, that a sudden dropping through up to the knee in slush is the first indication of their presence. It would be a very great advantage to take this treacherous part of the route before the effects of the night frost disappear, but it could only be done by leaving Chamonix about two or three in the morning.

In about four hours and a half from Chamonix, we reached the Jardin, which is probably one of the most singular spots in creation. Nearly in the centre of a vast crater—the base of which is a sea of ice about two miles in diameter, shut in by a barrier of lofty and tremendous peaks in every direction, excepting where the glacier finds its outlet down the icy cataract which I have endeavoured to describe— is a rocky island nearly covered with coarse mountain grasses, and an abundance of wild flowers, at an elevation of nearly ten thousand feet above the level of the sea. This is the mountain-garden, wonderful in itself, but possessing its greatest charm in the marvellous view which it commands. From the pure white surface of the glacier rise in sublime magnificence the Aiguille Verte, the Moine, the Lechaud, and the Aiguille sans Nom, connected by a complete chain of similar, though smaller peaks, except at the side towards the south-west, which seems expressly left open to show the grandest feature of all, the summit of Mont Blanc soaring above the vast plateau of the Glacier du Géant. The sensation of awful beauty which fills a thoughtful mind in contemplating such a scene is almost overpowering. Look at the last volume of Ruskin's " Modern Painters," and see how the mind of the poet-painter can commune with the wonders of the everlasting hills! and yet, firm and gigantic as they look, these, too, are not everlasting. Slab after slab of solid rock comes thundering down under the influences of alternate heat and cold, and those long lines of moraine mark accurately enough that it is only a question of time to bring down the proud mountain-tops and deposit them in the valley. The eye of a Lyell can trace the retrogression of Niagara fall for sixty thousand years marked on its barrier of rocks; and what changes may not such another period make among these obelisks of Nature — these landmarks of a Cyclopean world!

The blaze of the sun was dazzling, but while we watched the glorious spectacle, a thin white cloud formed upon the glacier, and, growing as it went, sailed across to the superior attractions of Mont Blanc, the upper part of which was soon concealed from our view. After enjoying an hour upon the Jardin, we recrossed the Taléfre glacier, and rapidly descended towards Chamonix, where we arrived at about four in the afternoon, having spent a day which can never be forgotten. Between the Aiguille Verte and the Aiguille sans Nom, there is a long barrier of very formidable-looking rocky points called Les Droites and Les Tours des Courtes: these are generally considered impassable, but a great many expeditions long considered impracticable have nevertheless been accomplished in the Alpine regions;

and, if a way can be found across this barrier, a descent would at once be made upon the glacier of Argentière, and a most interesting circuit to Chamonix be completed; very possibly the difficulty may be insuperable, but I cannot help thinking it may be well worth while for a determined party of good climbers to see what can be done in that direction with the aid of a good rope.

On a perfectly beautiful day we ascended the Brevent, and found that, with not more than average walking, we reached the summit in less than three hours; and, including an hour and a half there, we were not more than seven hours in completing the expedition and returning to Chamonix — a result which rather surprised us, as "Murray's Handbook" devoted twelve hours to it, and even hinted at the advisableness of sleeping at the Châlet of Plianpraz, than which it would be difficult to conceive a more wretched resting-place, as the wind whistles completely through it, and the proprietress herself confessed that, at the beginning of each summer season, her first task is to clear out the snow with which it is half filled. The only remarkable part of the ascent is a place called the Cheminée, where small footsteps have been cut on the face of a nearly perpendicular rock for about thirty or forty feet. With the steps there is no particular difficulty, but when I was first at Chamonix, there was a story of an adventurous lady who stuck in the middle, in a fit of hysterics, and could neither be got up nor down till revived by a libation of cognac, after which she successfully completed the ascent.

By the time we were ready to leave the top, after feasting on the glorious view of the great mountain, white mist was gathering on the side towards Chamonix. The summit of the Brevent consists on that side of steep precipices terminating in a sharp edge, but on the other side the inclination is more gradual: and here we saw a remarkable phenomenon, which is also mentioned by Mr. Wills as having been seen in the neighbourhood of the Hörnli. Looking towards Chamonix, the sun and wind were both behind us, and the latter prevented the cloud from rolling over the summit; under these circumstances we each saw a perfect double circular rainbow in the mist, with our own image in the centre, moving in answer to every movement of our limbs. Another party with guides was on the summit with us, and all thought it a very wonderful and unusual thing to find themselves thus drawn and framed in a rainbow by a novel kind of photography.

After we had made several other expeditions

around Chamonix, my old friend Jean Tairraz reappeared in the village, having been away with another party for several days. I had seen him first at Zermatt, in 1854, and, having been extremely pleased with him, I was very glad to see him again, and agreed to try if I could not melt the heart of the *chef des guides* to let him go with us, even though out of his turn on the *rôle*. That functionary, however, was inexorable; and though I represented to him, which was the fact, that Tairraz was a naturalist, and that I wanted his society and services in that capacity, "pour chercher des fleurs et des minéraux," rather than as a guide in a district whose bearings were now so familiar to me, all was of no avail; and I was obliged to authorise my friend Jean, by means of bribery and corruption, to effect an exchange of turns with the man who was first on the list. This was soon arranged, and Jean returned to announce with great delight that he was at our service. Young Proment returned to Courmayeur very well satisfied with a good week's employment in our company. We had every reason to be most highly satisfied with him; but as he did not profess to know anything about the Buet, which we wished to ascend, we had less scruple in changing him for the experience of Jean Tairraz.

On the next day the weather was not considered fine enough for an expedition to the Buet, which must extend over one day; but we determined to have a day's walk somewhere with Jean. We started off to the Pelérins cascade, and then climbed up by the same route that is taken for the first part of the ascent to Mont Blanc, with the intention of going as far as the weather might permit. We climbed through the region of wood and then emerged upon rough stony slopes, rapidly ascending till at last we came to what is called the Pierre Pointue. Those who make use of mules to save themselves from being fatigued in the upper part of the great ascent are obliged to part with them at this point, and trust to the strength and energy of themselves or their guides, as the case may be. The mist continued to thicken, but we resolved to push on, in the hope of finding matters better in the upper regions : the path turns to the right and winds along the face of precipitous rocks, sometimes almost hanging over the Glacier des Bossons, and there are some giddy heads which would find this part of the way no small obstacle in the ascent of Mont Blanc. Among the rocks on the sides, I here found several specimens of a pure white gentian, which I have never seen anywhere else, and which certainly puzzled the botanical old woman who inhabited the châlet of the Pelérins.

Some rough walking and climbing brought us presently to the Pierre de l'Échelle, the resting-place of the ladder which is used for crossing to the Grands Mulets. On we went, with Excelsior for our watchword, without any definite notion of what our expedition might terminate in, but resolved to see something of the upper part of the Bossons.

We all felt some of a poacher's excitement as we began to trespass with our unpretending party of three upon the sacred regions of the " Grande course par excellence"; our spirits rose with our bodies, and, in spite of all the terrors of the Chamonix *règlement*, which would have compelled us to take four guides instead of one, I really think we should have made a dash at the Grands Mulets, if the weather had improved, and paid the fine for Jean afterwards.

Higher up, Jean made rather a sudden halt, and, pointing up to the wall-like end of a small steep glacier from the Aiguille du Midi, still some distance above us to the left, he shook his head, and remarked, "C'est une mauvaise place là-haut!" the danger consisting in the great falls of ice which constantly descend right across the path we were now taking.

Presently we came to the edge of a broad sloping gully in the mountain-side, leading from the icy precipice overhead to the glacier below: this was covered with the *débris* of recent ice-falls, and was evidently their regular line of march: huge blocks weighing several tons were mixed up with beds of smaller fragments, and the sharp edges and freshly broken surfaces showed clearly that a fall had recently taken place; Jean therefore occupied himself a few moments in looking up at the state of the ice overhead, to see if any more was likely to come down at the wrong moment for us, and then saying that we might cross, and adding, "Mais il faut passer vite!" he led the way very rapidly over the mass of ruin, and in a few moments we had passed the worst part of it. The Glacier des Bossons was close to us, and we could not help getting a little way upon it. But there was no more to be done: the mist settled into steady rain, and if we had advanced far on the glacier, we might have had considerable trouble in finding our way back again. The neighbourhood of the overhanging glacier with its long blue fissures threatening us from above was much too dangerous a place to wait in for fine weather, so we reluctantly abandoned the hope of getting any further, and made a rapid retreat from the rain, which began to fall very heavily, without having seen any of the splendid view which we depended upon.

We hurried down without stopping till we came to the Pelérins hut, and being exceedingly hungry, we enjoyed luncheon immensely, while the old woman showed us a capital collection of plants dried by herself; the sun came out again in about an hour, and we had just time to walk ourselves dry before arriving at Chamonix. As we walked through the noble forest of pines, many an old Cambridge recollection was revived, as I thought of the ubiquitous essence of the Eternal City, perpetuated in the scientific language which even that old Chamoniard peasant was forced to recognise in the Latin nomenclature of her plants. A few days after this we again started with Jean Tairraz to visit the series of glaciers which descend from the line of Aiguilles extending from the Charmoz to the Midi. Beginning with the regular Montanvert path, we turned to the right and continued a very steep ascent through the pine woods, till we came out on a rough rocky desert at the foot of the Nantillon glacier. Between this and the glacier de Blaitiére there is a vast gorge covered with the gigantic blocks brought down in rather dangerous frequency from the precipitous Aiguilles above. Some of these were almost as large as an ordinary house, and it was with some difficulty and much scrambling that I found my way among them to the left, while my less curious companions moved towards the Blaitiére on the right, where they agreed to wait for my arrival. Getting clear at last of this rocky wilderness, I found myself at the foot of the lofty moraine of the Nantillon glacier, up which I immediately climbed, and as my head overtopped the barrier, I had the great satisfaction of finding myself face to face with a pair of chamois, who, having no idea of being disturbed in a solitude seldom visited by man, were not more than eighty or a hundred yards from me, within an easy shot. They did not wait long, though, to see whether I was armed with " la longue carabine," but bounded up the higher part of the glacier, and, taking most scientific zigzags over a very steep bed of snow, were soon safely ensconced on the unapproachable precipices of the Aiguille, from which they looked down on me with an evident feeling of security. Crossing the moraine, I descended upon the glacier, which was tolerably easy to walk over, though if quite inexperienced in the glacier world I might have got into trouble among the wilderness of crevasses, sometimes partly and sometimes wholly filled up with fresh snow. If anyone unaccustomed to such places finds himself there alone, I would give him one caution which he will find a pretty certain rule of safety. Let him observe only the *colour* of the snow, and he will find that where it is rather brown it is always old and strong, while the white patches are generally more or less dangerous from their freshness.

After examining the glacier as much as I wished, I recrossed the stony wilderness towards the west, and, by rapid movements, managed to rejoin the rest of the party just as they were preparing to come to anchor at the side of the Blaitiére glacier. We selected a huge tabular rock, with a stream of pure melted snow by its side, for our dining-room: here we unpacked a cold chicken and some good wine from Jean's knapsack, with which we made a capital luncheon, in a spot commanding a magnificent view of the valley of Chamonix and the mountains on its northern side.

We then crossed the entire width of the Blaitiére glacier, and another rocky gorge which led us to the Glacier des Pelérins, after passing which in the same direction, we began to descend towards the Para châlet. Coming within the range of vegetation once more, we soon found ourselves at the top of such an exceedingly steep slope of ground covered with a mass of Alpine rhododendrons that it would have been impossible to walk down it, and we were on the point of turning to the right, to find a more practicable descent.

We solved the difficulty, however, by sitting down on the shrubby underwood, and in a rapid bumping *glissade* soon found ourselves several hundred feet down the side of the mountain, after which we crossed a rough gorge with a stream thundering along it, and prepared for a short halt with a pipe. Now, however, I found that my pipe was lost, and supposing that it had been jolted out of my pocket in the rough descent, I went back with Tairraz to search for it. Of course there was no path, but up we went, tracing our route by the disturbance of the bushes. The pipe was not to be found, but in returning I found a handsome porte-monnaie which belonged, as I knew, to one of my companions, and contained cards, cigars, a letter of credit, and 200 francs in cash. This was a lucky discovery, for as we were quite out of the way of any beaten track, the lost treasure would probably not have been found for many years, and its owner would have known nothing of his loss until we reached Chamonix, when recovery would have been hopeless. This excursion is very seldom made, but its roughness is most fully compensated for by the interesting insight which it gives of the upper and secondary glaciers, at an elevation of from 8000 to 9000 feet above the sea. Passing close to the foot of the precipitous Aiguilles of Charmoz, Grépon, and Blaitiére, one is fully enabled to judge of and admire their magnificent structure, and from a spot called the Plan des Aiguilles, there is a view which must be almost equal to that from the Grands Mulets. The expedition may very easily be performed in about seven or eight hours, but it is fully worth while to spend a long day upon it.

CHAP. XII.

Start for the Buet. — Argentière. — A new Route. — View from the Summit. — A singular Line of Descent. — Pierre de Berar. — Glacier des Bossons. — Montanvert and the Mauvais Pas. — An American on Foot. — Wonderful Effect of Moonlight.

MEANWHILE, serener skies set in, and Jean declaring that the weather was "assuré," we determined on our long-talked-of expedition to the Buet. Two ways from Chamonix were open to us; the one occupying two days and a half, the other little more than one day. As the season was late in September, we determined on the latter course by Argentière, instead of going round by Servoz and the Col d'Anterne. Accordingly, on a fine Sunday afternoon, we started with Jean and arrived at Argentière in an hour and a half from Chamonix, telling the landlord to keep our rooms, as we intended to return on the following day.

Close to the station of the *douaniers*, we found

a new inn, in the châlet style, of which the landlord was justly proud, as he and his son had collected the whole of the materials themselves. It was quite new, and the bed-rooms were not yet habitable, so, after a comfortable little supper, we were escorted to a small house in the village, where we were to sleep. Jean turned into bed in the adjoining room, after giving orders that we should be called at three in the morning. He was awake early, and, as our baggage for one night consisted of nothing but a couple of tooth-brushes and a comb between us, we were soon on foot, and by the aid of a candle found our way to the inn. Here we discovered the landlady, an old squaw of portentous dimensions and ugliness, busily occupied in preparing breakfast for us; her good-nature was equal to her bulk, and that is saying not a little in her praise; but we found breakfast progressing very slowly; so we went with Jean to the kitchen, with the view of giving personal assistance in the operations. We found the old lady busily peering over various utensils of strange form, among which she had managed to puzzle herslf so completely, that she seemed to forget their respective contents. Consequently, on bringing the various articles to light, with Jean's active aid, we found that the eggs were as hard as the Aiguille du Midi, while the coffee had only endured the few minutes' boiling which was due to the eggs. Anything, however, would do under the circumstances; and, with the help of some unexceptionable honey, we fared famously. There was still some delay in packing up the day's provisions, but at last we started, about half-past four, on as fine a morning as ever was seen.

Leaving the path to the Col de Balme on our right, we took that of the Tête Noire, which we followed till within a short distance of Valorsine. We then diverged to the left over a rough swampy ground intersected by numerous small watercourses, among which it was difficult to pick our way in the dark; but before we were fairly in the Val de Berar, the first symptoms of dawn appeared, lighting up the ferruginous peaks of the Aiguilles Rouges with a splendid tinge of carmine; the stars soon disappeared, and as we entered the narrow gorge near a beautiful waterfall, every sign of a perfectly fine day greeted us most cheerily.

The Val de Berar is very narrow and confined, and the unusually heavy snow of the preceding winter was still lying in many large deep beds at the bottom of it; and their retarding effect upon vegetation was very pleasingly conspicuous in masses of the rosy-blossomed rhododendrons actually growing out of the snow, in full bloom at least two months after most of them had ceased to flower in warmer situations. The ordinary route to the Buet leads far up this valley before turning to the right so as to ascend by a gradual course over gently sloping beds of snow to the summit; and Jean had told us that seven hours of good walking would be required to reach it from Argentière: but after going for several miles up the valley, we came to another large bed of snow, stretching completely across it, just above which a few shepherds were tending their flocks. Here we happened to cast a glance up the mountain on our right, where a very steep slope terminated in a formidable row of precipitous rocks several thousand feet above us. I knew that this was exactly in the direction of the Buet, though it was still concealed from us, and I asked Jean if it might not possibly be approached directly from where we were, instead of by the usual roundabout course: he shook his head at first, saying that no one had ever tried the ascent in that way, and confessing that he knew nothing as to its practicability. However, he spoke to the shepherds, who said they knew the ridge of rocks overhead might be reached, though they knew nothing beyond: we at once determined on the experiment, and inviting two lads to join us, we climbed straight up over rocky ground mixed with a good deal of mountain grass and small bushes. We arrived at the ridge, and finding a means of passing the barrier of rocks, we saw that our geographical notion was correct: we were exactly face to face with the Buet, only separated from us by a huge kind of crater, over which its snowy summit towered.

The eastern side of the crater on our right terminated in a high rocky ridge or *arête*, and we at once resolved to make for this. The climbing was rather severe, as the footing consisted of a loose black shale inclined at a steep angle, and resembled a vast mound of loose small coal, which gave way at every step: patience and determination, however, overcame the obstacle, though I could not help being amused by the puffing and groaning of the shepherds, who kept exclaiming, "Ah! ça est fatigant." The moment we reached the top of the ridge, the view which I had anticipated burst upon us; in an instant the Dent du Midi and the whole group of the Oberland mountains were before us.

Up to this point we had been not quite four hours from Argentière, and we calculated that another half hour would take us to the top. All were in the highest possible spirits, for it was now evident that our new route, though rather difficult, was very considerably shorter and better than the ordinary course; and we at once determined to wait and have our second meal upon the ridge, before we ascended the snowy cupola of the mountain. Our shepherd companions had some black bread and cheese of their own, but were highly delighted by a taste of our more dainty fare, especially as it was washed down with a glass of good Burgundy; and after half an hour's delay we moved on along the narrow ridge towards the north. A lofty wall-like excrescence of jagged rock threatened to stop us; but, in spite of Jean's cautious remonstrances, I clambered up it, followed by one of the peasants, and we gazed a good quarter of an hour upon the rest of the party, who preferred descending some distance and climbing up again over the loose shale before they could turn the obstacle and rejoin us.

Meanwhile I advanced to the foot of the icy bed which crowns the summit of the Buet, my companion still entertaining me with his accompaniment of groans. After a few steps on soft snow I found myself on a steep bed of hard ice, which might easily be climbed with the aid of an axe to cut steps, but proved quite impracticable without it. In vain I tried to advance slowly, making notches in the ice with the point of my alpenstock, and standing as firm as I could. It proved an impossible task, as Jean at once discovered when he came in sight with the rest of the party. I was obliged to return cautiously, and a brief council of war decided that we had only two courses open to us: one of these was to descend a long way, and, by means of a great circuit, join the usual route to the top; the other, to climb by the edge of the ice, which absolutely overhung a tremendous precipice on the right. We determined to try the latter, which was more hazardous, but infinitely shorter than the former; Jean led the way, with the elder shepherd behind him, followed by Dundas and myself, the younger shepherd preferring to wait till he saw we could succeed. We each went down on the right knee, holding the alpenstock firmly in the left hand, whilst the right hand was employed in clutching the very edge of the icy wall, which was fortunately covered by a thin wreath of fresh snow a few inches in width.

Slowly, but steadily, we ascended about a hundred feet, when Dundas lost his hold by the right hand, and instantly slid down like a flash of lightning over the immense incline of ice on the left. At first I was greatly alarmed, but with great presence of mind and command of his alpenstock, he managed to keep his feet foremost, and we had the great satisfaction of seeing him stopped far below us by the soft snow, before he reached the rocks which would have given him a very rough reception. He instantly recovered himself from the mass of snow which nearly smothered him, and called out to us that he was not hurt: it was, however, impossible for him to re-ascend by the same way; and followed by the young shepherd, who did not seem to like the precipice, he made a circuit so as to join us on the top. We crawled up successfully, the most difficult place being the last, where was a great mass of overhanging wreathed snow, through which we had to make our way with the utmost caution, as a large hole in it showed us the full extent of the awful chasm below. With the aid of an axe and rope, this is undoubtedly the best way of ascending the Buet: without them it is very decidedly dangerous, and Tairraz said that he would not have thought of trying it, could he have seen what it was before we got to the middle: he had been six times on the summit of Mont Blanc, and said, that what we had just done was nearly as bad as the " Mur de la Côte sans haches."

I do not think it would have been possible to

climb up the edge as we did, if there had not been a slight depression in the ice, like a gutter, about three inches in width and one in depth, close to it, and parallel to its direction, which afforded a slight support to the knee, whilst the right hand grasped its very extremity, and actually projected over a precipice of whose depth I could form no idea, as the head could not stretch over far enough to enable one to look fairly down it without great danger. It was a great pity we had not brought an axe with us; for a quarter of an hour spent in cutting steps up the slope on the left would have made the ascent perfectly simple; but as the usual course offers a very gradual rise, we had not thought of any extra assistance.

The summit of the mountain consists of a splendid field of pure ice, partly sprinkled with snow, though the height is only about 10,000 feet. Here we all assembled after a little delay, and all trouble was forgotten in contemplating one of the most splendid panoramas that can be conceived. Those of us who had mounted by the ledge arrived on the highest point exactly at half-past nine, having thus been only five hours from Argentière, including half an hour for breakfast on the *arête*. Our route, therefore, had the advantage of shortness as well as novelty; and I should strongly recommend future visitors to take an axe, and follow our example.

The only vestige of a cloud in the whole sky was a low white mist which obstinately persisted in hiding the part of the Lake of Geneva which we ought to have seen. But far above and beyond this, the mountains on the north of the lake, as far as the distant Jura, were very beautifully distinct. Turning to the east, the Dent du Midi was our nearest conspicuous neighbour, over a shoulder of which the eye might leap at a glance to the peculiar conical tops of the Stokhorn range near the Lake of Thun, some fifty or sixty miles distant.

The whole range of the Bernese Alps was perfectly distinct, the dark parts softened by distance, while the snowy crowns of the Altels, the Breithorn, the Jungfrau, Mönch, and Finsteraarhorn, glittered like silver in the glorious sunshine. Running nearly from our feet, the whole valley of the Rhone lay stretched out before us, and more than a hundred miles of the winding river could be clearly traced, like a waving white thread, to its distant birthplace in the bosom of the Galenstok.

Further to the south, and separated by the Rhone valley from the mountains of the north, rose all the peaks of that giant group which extends from the Weisshorn to Monte Rosa, including the familiar forms of the Mischabel, the Dent Blanche, and the wondrous Matterhorn, which combined in forming a magnificent feature in the panorama, at a distance of from fifty to sixty miles.

Nearer to us, in the same direction, were the Velan and Combin, the giants of the St. Bernard, and the whole range of peaks between them and the Cervin. Close to our feet were the green undulating mountains which surround the Col de Balme with every variety of form. The small white house on the top of the pass was clearly seen, and just beyond the Col we looked right down upon the recesses of the white Glacier du Tour, over which Forbes once crossed the chain to Orsières.

The lower part of the glacier of Argentière was hidden by the intervening mass of the Aiguilles Rouges, and then far above the Brévent range, now dwindled into comparative nothingness, rose the vast forms of the Dome du Gouté and Mont Blanc. Never till then had I been able to form a just idea of the magnificence of "Le Mont Blanc," as the Chamoniards delight to call it. At this distance of fifteen miles it looks infinitely higher and grander than when seen from the nearer and more commonly visited points of view. Far up into the deep blue sky rose the dazzling whiteness of its summit, completely dwarfing the vast and elegant aiguilles which surround its base, and which appear almost as lofty as itself when seen from the neighbourhood of the valley. Finding how great a distance was necessary to show it in perfection, we were enabled to form a proper idea of the immensity of the mountain.

Beyond all comparison, the Buet is the finest point for observing it; and the awful grandeur of the higher parts of the panorama is charmingly relieved by the vast variety of green valleys and undulating hills which form the nearer and lower portion of it, bathed, as we saw them, in a warmth of light and colour quite indescribable by the most enthusiastic poet.

After remaining till 11 o'clock in the full enjoyment of the scene, we dismissed our two shepherd lads with a few francs; and, leaving them astonished and delighted with their adventure, we struck out a course for our descent to the north of that which we had taken in the morning, descending over a series of very long slopes of snow *en glissade*, which we were now experienced enough to accomplish in the true Chamonix fashion, standing up with the feet close together, and leaning back on the long *bâton*, which is used like a rudder. Our line of descent was quite original; beyond the general direction, nobody knew anything about it; and sometimes it was necessary to stop the *glissade* as suddenly as possible, on finding the snow-beds terminate abruptly in a narrow funnel between the rocks, where they were undermined by rushing watercourses. Great caution was observed on these occasions; but at length we found ourselves fairly committed to a considerable difficulty. The last snow ended in a very narrow gorge, through which a large stream of water descended in a noisy cascade upon the rocks below. To go back would have been a long and vexatious proceeding, and there was no way of going forward, except by climbing down a high wall of rocks close to the side of the cascade, which covered them with its spray. Jean thought we could not possibly pass this obstacle; but knowing the shortness of his legs, I led the way, and scrambled safely down to the bottom, whence I found that, by clinging to some tough rhododendrons, I could turn the corner of the rocky wall at a point from which further descent by the watercourse was impossible. Delighted with this success, I returned to assist my companions, and we all found ourselves safely through our difficulties, and landed on a point, from which a run down the grassy slopes soon brought us to the Pierre de Berar, near the head of the valley.

This is a gigantic block, brought down from above, and we found a man occupied in building a hut at its side, so as to use the stone for the rear of his edifice, which he expected to make into a resting-place for travellers. It was very amusing to hear his oaths and expressions of astonishment as Jean told him of our new method of ascending and descending the Buet, and after contributing a franc to his lonely work, we moved down the valley to Argentière, turning aside to visit a fine waterfall a little above Valorsine.

The old landlord at Argentière was astonished at our early return; and, after paying his bill, we walked on at a rapid pace to Chamonix, arriving there at four in the afternoon, many hours sooner than we were expected. The length of this expedition is considerable, as the base of the Buet is fifteen or sixteen miles from Chamonix, and nearly ten from Argentière, in addition to which the ascent is steep and in parts fatiguing. But I know of no excursion in which, with fine weather, all trouble is more completely compensated for by the charm and the variety of the panorama from the summit.

However long the day's work may be, good training appears to remove the possibility of fatigue, and we were up at the usual hour in the morning ready for another expedition. Jean did not appear according to custom, about breakfast-time, so we wandered about the village for a while, amusing ourselves with looking into the windows of the *magasins*, filled with prints, crystals, dried plants, carved wood, and all the pretty things so well known to everyone who has visited Chamonix. The season was drawing to a close, and groups of guides, with nothing to do beyond lounging about at the corners, gave a very picturesque appearance to the village; though, as we looked at some of them, we could not help thinking that many visitors must have thought the regulation of the *rôle* rather unsatisfactory.

Still there was no sign of Jean, and, thinking that he must be knocked up, we determined to go out for a walk, and inquire after him in the evening. We did not wish to go far, as we rather expected some friends to arrive from Geneva or Sallenches in the afternoon; so we took the well-known path to the Pelérins, and thence pushed our way through the beautiful masses of rhododendrons, ferns, and mossy rocks under the fir-woods, towards the Glacier des Bossons. Arriving at the lofty moraine, we scrambled over it, and found ourselves on that exquisitely pure region of ice. This glacier is, as the Chamoniards call it, " si propre," and the whiteness of the ice so dazzling, that it requires some little time before the eye can well distinguish the inequalities of the surface, a knowledge of which is necessary to secure a proper footing.

The ice is much harder and smoother than on most glaciers, and, at the point where we reached it, consists of long undulations, each of which is covered with a kind of ripple, as if the ocean had been suddenly frozen when a gentle breeze was playing upon a long swell.

We picked our way across it, and gradually descended to the right, till we found ourselves in a maze of huge crevasses and pinnacles, among which it was utterly impossible to move further without the aid of a ladder. Vast caverns of intense blue divide the torn masses and pinnacles of ice, which vary in colour from the purest white on their summit to a deep blue in the crevasses from which they spring. Some of them were as sharp and lofty as a Gothic steeple, others, huge shapeless monsters, tumbled about in all directions; and here and there could be seen the mangled remains of a giant pile, cast down from dignity by the onward movement of the glacier, and pouring out of every crack the frigid essence of its life, which dripped from its melting carcase under the powerful influence of the sun.

We thought of exploring the higher part of the glacier, but gathering clouds in that direction warned us that there would be very little comfort or satisfaction in such an experiment, and promised one of those days which, on the mountains, have so often reminded me of Tennyson's exquisite description in the "Two Voices," where he compares the hopelessness of man's attempting to arrive at the true sources of wisdom and the essence of knowledge, to his wanderings on a mountain obscured by mists : —

> " Cry, faint not, climb : the summits slope
> Beyond the furthest flights of hope,
> Wrapt in dense cloud from base to cope.
>
> " Sometimes a little corner shines,
> As over rainy mist inclines
> A gleaming crag with belts of pines.
>
> " I will go forward, sayest thou,
> I shall not fail to find her now ;
> Look up ! the fold is on her brow.
>
> " If straight thy path, or if oblique,
> Thou know'st not, shadows thou dost strike,
> Embracing cloud, Ixion-like."

We made no further attempt at ascending, but contented ourselves with a quiet ramble in the luxuriant woods; and after spending half an hour in the study of botany with the old lady of the Pelérins, we returned to Chamonix.

In the evening we were joined by the ladies who had arrived from Sallenches, and about the same time Jean made his appearance, with rather a crestfallen look, attributing his absence to a severe lumbago. The fact is, that Jean is not so young as he used to be, and the Buet journey had been rather too rapid for him.

We now constituted him director-general of excursions for the ladies, with full powers to obtain mules, and get the necessary number of assistants for visiting the Flegère, Col de Voza, Montanvert, and Mer de Glace. These expeditions occupied several days very pleasantly, and the whole party successfully crossed the glacier from the Montanvert house to the Chapeau, descending by the narrow path called the Mauvais Pas. This path is really difficult to those not accustomed to such work: cut out upon the face of the rocks, it is so narrow, that it is impossible for one person to pass by another without either ascending or descending, so as to turn the position. Walking first, I found in the middle of it an unfortunate American gentleman, positively on all fours, wriggling down like a worm, covered with dirt, and speechless with fear of falling over upon the glacier some hundred feet below. He would not stand upright, and it was impossible to help him; moreover, he filled up the path; and finding it impossible to crawl after him at such a slow pace, I clambered up the surface of the rocks on the right, and holding on by clefts and bushes, I succeeded in completely outflanking him, and descending on the path some little way below where he still " dragged his slow length along."

The ladies behaved admirably; and we finished a most agreeable day by descending the remainder of the path to where their mules were waiting, whence we soon returned to Chamonix. Several more days were spent in the same pleasant way; and then the time came for breaking up the party. Dundas and his friends were going southwards, towards Florence, and I had to settle with myself as to the best way of returning to England. I had thought of going to Geneva and Paris, and was beginning to groan inwardly at the thought of long journeys in a diligence, when a happy notion struck me, and I resolved to leave by the Col de Balme, and work my way once more through the most charming scenery of Switzerland.

The last evening I spent at Chamonix was marked by one of the most wonderful sights I have ever seen, — an effect of moonlight never to be forgotten. The moon was rising just behind the Aiguille du Midi, and though hidden by that huge and lofty mass, was pouring its light full upon the summit of Mont Blanc and the Dome du Gouté through the intervening space. The whole canopy of snow was bathed in a silvery light, which all round the edge became as brilliant as the moon itself, while, in marvellous contrast to this side of the picture, a vast black fan-like shadow from the Aiguille du Midi, stretched upwards into the starry heaven. The whole effect was almost unearthly in its sublimity, and even the Chamoniards, accustomed as they are to scenes of grandeur, turned out of their houses in the greatest excitement.

CHAP. XIII.

Departure from Chamonix. — The Col de Balme. — Martigny. — An enthusiastic Engineer. — Lombard Sportsmen. — Sion. — Ayent. — Passage of the Rawyl. — Singular Cascades. — The Wildstrubel. — Beauties of the Simmenthal. — Ander Lenk.

WE had spent a fortnight in the valley of Chamonix, and, though the weather had not been uniformly fine, we had never been kept in for the whole day. The great variety of excursions in the neighbourhood may easily occupy a longer time than this, and, after all, we had neither crossed the Col du Géant nor made the ascent of Mont Blanc.

And what a pleasant place it is — this Chamonix — provided you are not there at the very height of the season, when quarters can only be obtained with difficulty. There are always some agreeable people to be found in the hotels, though, unfortunately, there are generally some exceptions. We made many acquaintances, and amongst them that of Mr.

Coleman, an artist as well as a mountaineer, who has now made three ascents of Mont Blanc, for the purpose of obtaining original sketches. In the first ascent he failed in arriving at the highest point, partly through the misconduct of a guide; but on two subsequent occasions he has been perfectly successful, and his interesting and valuable drawings are being lithographed on a large and handsome scale.

Early on the morning of Sunday, the 23rd of September, I said good-bye to my friends, and started off alone for Martigny by the Col de Balme. Walking briskly on, I soon came to Argentière, and had a parting word with the old couple of the inn; their next neighbours, the *douaniers*, were satisfied in their turn, and another half hour brought me to the village of Le Tour, where I was surprised at coming up with a party of peasants whom I had seen leave Chamonix more than an hour before me. From this point a long bleak ascent, very steep in parts, led me to the house on the top of the Col. Up to this point I had refused to look back at the view of the valley; but, now upon the summit, I turned round and saw spread out before me all the line of woods, glaciers, and aiguilles, which alternately display their charms until barred out by the

Col de Voza. I had been walking three hours and a quarter from Chamonix, and I spent an hour in the enjoyment of the view from the top, after which I walked down the long descent to Trient, the lower part of the way being among a pine forest, where men were busy felling timber. At the foot of this there was a large green tract of pasture-land, as smooth as a cricket-ground, and decked with a great profusion of the purple autumn crocus in full bloom. The ascent of the Col de Trient was soon completed, being a very trifling affair when compared with the Col de Balme.

The authorities of the Canton Valais are very anxious to get something out of everyone coming from the south, and a *gensdarme* spends the whole of the year in a small house on the Col de Trient, where he inspects passports, and demands a franc for doing so. He is a capital fellow, and keeps a small store of provisions for travellers: in winter time he must be sometimes in need of them all for himself and his wife, as the snow occasionally nearly buries his house, and makes the path impassable for several days together.

A few steps further, and the valley of the Rhone is seen stretching away in front and far below, the river narrowing into a slender thread, as we had seen it in the same direction from the Buet; and far above the long range of inferior mountains that flank the northern side of the valley, the Diablerets, the Strubel, and the great Oberland peaks, lift their snowy summits to the sky. A charming walk of nearly two hours from the top of the Col de Trient brought me to Martigny, the latter half of the way passing among magnificent chestnuts and walnuts, with a considerable quantity of smaller fruit-trees. Fruit, however, has been a dangerous thing to meddle with, ever since the days of Adam; and I paid the penalty of rashness by being set upon by a swarm of wasps, which fairly made me take to my heels after being stung severely on the hand.

Martigny is a busy place in the travelling season, standing as it does at the junction of four frequented routes, the road to Geneva in one direction, and to the Simplon in the other, besides the mountain paths to Chamonix and the Great St. Bernard. I never, however, heard of anyone staying there long, though the hotels are well fitted as sleeping-places. The situation is hot and low, and the immediate neighbourhood of the Rhone has given the town an unpleasant reputation for musquitoes. The road and the river are as nearly as possible on a level, and the alluvial soil of the vicinity appears extremely fertile, maize especially growing in very great luxuriance. The whole country looks as if it must be terribly subject to inundations; but yet I believe the Rhone does not often burst its bounds very seriously. On the walls of some houses in the town, however, a mark about twelve or fourteen feet above the road shows the height to which the water rose some years ago, when the waters of the Dranse, having been long dammed up by ice in the valley towards the St. Bernard, broke loose at last, and, after deluging Martigny, and doing an incredible amount of damage, were carried away by the Rhone.

The bustle of the season was now over, and in the handsome Hôtel de la Tour I only found two men, who joined me in a pleasant supper. One of them was a Lombard, who had been driven from his home, at Milan, by the cholera; and the other was a very entertaining Polish engineer, who was fixed at Martigny for some time while arranging for the commencement of the railway which is to connect the Lake of Geneva with the Simplon Pass. We passed a very agreeable evening together, as we could all speak French tolerably. Though both my friends probably had a common topic in their detestation of Austria, yet they did not seem to like talking politics, and that ground was soon abandoned. The Lombard gave us dreadful accounts of the cholera in the cities south of the Alps, where many factories were closed from the masters losing a large proportion of their men; and the engineer, warming with his own subject, showed himself a wonderful enthusiast in railways.

Presently he insisted upon taking us out for a walk by moonlight up the valley, to see where the first ground had been broken for the new line. So we lighted cigars, and walked along the straight road towards Sion, he talking all the way about the nature and capabilities of the soil, and of a peculiar usage which the inhabitants have of fertilising it with an application of sand. After walking three miles, he turned off to the left of the main road, to show us the commencement of his hobby, the railroad, the moon being bright enough for us to distinguish the ground marked out, with the beginning of a low embankment. The construction of this line will be easy enough as far as Brieg; but to take it over the Simplon with thirteen kilometres of tunnels through the rock, will be indeed a work of difficulty.

He seemed full of confidence, however, and told us an amusing story of how he had astonished the young king of Portugal, who happened to be crossing the Simplon just as my friend was engaged in making observations on the pass. His Majesty, whom he persisted in calling "ce petit gamin," had alighted from his carriage, and asked what he was doing, upon which the unblushing Pole replied that he was engaged in the construction of a railway from Lisbon to Calcutta! He proceeded to justify his extravagance by explaining to us a system of railroads, by which he calculated that all the capitals of Europe would be easily connected directly with the cities of the East. Upon our expressing some doubts of its realisation, he broke out into a rhapsodical description of a sort of coming millennium of *chemins de fer*, adding, "Mais, ma foi, messieurs, nous allons faire un chemin de fer jusqu'à Paradis, et quand le vieux diable voudra voyager par le convoi, l'Archange Michel, avec le glaive dans sa main, le chassera hors de la station!" After this outburst he stopped, partly to enjoy a good laugh at his own idea, and partly for want of breath, after which he went on more quietly, and after a very pleasant evening we arrived at the hotel, not much before eleven at night.

The first noise I heard in the morning was caused by the Lombard and his goods being packed upon a mule, and starting on the way to Chamonix: for, like nearly all foreigners, he had a most complete horror of walking far. I had only to walk to Sion over eighteen or twenty miles of flat road, and therefore was in no hurry to start. At last I set off upon the first stage of nine miles, which is as straight as a mathematical line, on a dead level, with the certainty of Martigny church at one end, and a large white building in Riddes at the other end, being visible throughout the whole way. My only object was to reverse their apparent distances, and, as I left mile after mile behind me, the church looked smaller and Riddes became more distinct. The heat was tremendous; the ground was covered with grasshoppers, of all sorts and colours, leaping about in every direction and knocking their heads together in mid-air; the very frogs, in spite of their cold internal arrangements, were evidently in the condition of the "perspiring" member of their species immortalised by an ode in "Pickwick," and made desperate leaps into the ditches as, one by one, they found the land unbearable. The only creature apparently at all comfortable was a man engaged in cutting rushes, up to his middle in a swamp, who laughed when I congratulated him on his situation.

At length I came to the end of the most detestable piece of road I have ever been foolish enough to walk over, and turned into the dirty little inn at Riddes to get some shade and refreshment. Some peasants were doing the same; everything was of the roughest: but I sat down at a table with three men, who had guns and dogs by their side, and powder-flasks on a bench. We saluted one another, and I soon found that they were Lombards who had crossed the mountains on a shooting excursion. Their dogs consisted of a tolerably good-looking pointer and a half-bred setter, the bleeding head of the latter looking uncommonly as if he had been shot by mistake.

The owner of the pointer had been in England at the Great Exhibition, and was highly delighted when, upon being appealed to, I declared that the dog was, indeed, a veritable pointer, such as we have in England. I asked what sport they had had, upon which one of them produced two small birds wrapped up in the leaf of a cabbage, attributing their want of success to the heat of the day. Presently something was said about politics, and, upon my expressing an opinion in favour of Italian independence, they all rose together, and insisted, with the greatest enthusiasm, on drinking my health in another bottle of wine. We then parted as the best possible friends, and they went forth into the fields in hopes of better sport, while I continued my way to Sion, where I arrived just in time to escape drenching from a sudden thunder-shower.

At the Hôtel de la Poste, I found the most obliging landlord I have ever met with on the Continent; he seemed really devoted to studying my convenience, and charged less than I have anywhere paid, except in the remotest villages. I told him that I wished to cross the Rawyl pass to Lenk in the Simmenthal, and he promised that he would try and find a guide for me, adding, however, that it would not be very easy, as the pass was not much frequented. In the course of the evening, he said he had not found anyone who knew the whole of the pass, but introduced to me a little man whose regular business is carrying letters and messages; and who offered to take me to the village of Ayent, about two hours' walk, where he knew of a man who would take me over the Rawyl. By all accounts, it was likely to be a long day's work, and arrangements were made for an early start. I did not, however, get breakfast till six o'clock, and we did not move fairly off until half an hour later.

The landlord had packed up a small bundle of cold meat and bread, with a bottle of good wine, as there was not the slightest chance of our finding anything fit to eat till late in the evening. Martin, my little guide, carried this, and I took my own knapsack. The rain of the last night had made the fields, lanes, and orchards exceedingly dirty; but Martin knew all the short cuts, and lightened the way by continual gossip about the surrounding lands, houses, and mountains, the difficulties of life in general, and the many sorrows of himself, a "pauvre garçon," in particular. He was a whining old fellow, with nothing serious to complain of, that I could discover, and I was not sorry to arrive at Ayent, where I was to find my mountain-guide. This village is to the north-east of Sion, and, I should think, rather more than 1500 feet above it: its situation, among fine wood, is charming, and commands an extensive view of the Rhone valley and the dark mountains beyond. We arrived there at nine, the extreme heaviness of the ground having kept us rather longer than we expected. Up to this point there had been considerable doubt whether the clouds would permit me to cross the mountains; and Martin, whose mind was of the nervous order, kept shaking his head in a very alarming manner; but as we approached the village, I began to see a warm light spreading far and wide in the south, and peak after peak of the snowy mountains in that direction stood out in clear sunshine : the light drew nearer and nearer to us, and before long the woods of the mountain side, that sloped from our feet towards the valley of the Rhone, were glowing with warmth, as the last of the mist curled away in thin white wreaths. This gradual unfolding of the scene around us and below would alone have rewarded me for the dirty walk from Sion; but the victorious progress of sunshine seemed to promise that, though long clouds were still sailing across the mountains where the route of the Rawyl lay, the last signs of bad weather would disappear in another hour.

We passed through the churchyard, reposing in the shade of a noble walnut tree, but disfigured with a huge and most revoltingly coloured crucifix, near which Martin took me into a neat white cottage, where he was received as an old friend by the good woman of the house. The husband soon appeared; a remarkably fine, tall, dark, Italian-looking man, of about forty years old. Both of them treated me with rather a dignified hauteur: he appeared to think he was doing me a favour by acting as my guide, and she by letting him do so. But in such an unfrequented village as Ayent, it is not uncommon to find a bold independence of character among the inhabitants, which along the more beaten ways has faded beneath the constantly corrupting influence of the tourist's gold. My new guide offered to go with me to the further side of the summit of the pass, so as to return to Ayent the same day, for four francs, or to go on the whole way to Lenk for six francs. He did not seem to care whether or no he went at all; but I was too glad of such an offer to allow it to pass, and the bargain was at once concluded.

He kept me waiting a short time while he put on a suit of thick clothes, not being quite so hopeful as myself about the weather; and then, after leaving orders for the family arrangements in case of his being two days absent, he led the way towards the upper forests, while poor little Martin trudged back towards Sion.

The taciturnity of my grim companion, and the utter coolness with which he ignored me entirely for about half an hour after starting, made me at first almost suspicious of him, and I began to calculate the chances of victory, if he should take it into his head to quarrel with me in the dreary solitudes of the Rawyl. It was, however, only a passing thought, of which I instantly felt ashamed, and after a time we began to understand each other a little better. I found that he was a carpenter by trade, a drum-major by profession, and a guide "par occasion" in his own neighbourhood. The Rawyl seemed rather a hobby with him; and he told me that he had himself carried up the poles which mark the route over the upper part of the pass.

We ascended in a north-easterly direction, through a region of noble pine woods, by a path which could scarcely have been found by a stranger, and at last arrived at a spot where, through the branches of the dark firs, we had an enchanting view of the far-distant mountains near Zermatt, rearing their white summits into the clear sky. The steady improvement of the weather made me feel sure of a successful day, though my drum-major still looked suspiciously at the clouds, which obstinately hung about the pass. Presently, turning to the left, we found ourselves on the edge of a vast amphitheatre in the mountains, closed on all sides except that by which we entered it, the lower part all clothed with a broad girdle of forest, the upper regions terminating in savage cliffs and precipices, which on our left rose from our feet to a vast height almost perpendicularly.

For a considerable distance the path had been cut out along the face of this, and was scarcely more than a foot wide, while a rushing stream often disputed even this narrow way with us; and in several places where the path was entirely monopolised by the water, we had to cross on a single pine-stem, about eight inches broad, stretched across from one point of rock to another, with nothing else to keep us from falling into the deep chasm on the right; and what with the fact of these bridges being very slippery from the spray, and of the stream rushing wildly past at the distance of only a few feet, we sometimes found it rather difficult for a few minutes to maintain our precarious position. A little further, this path became even worse, for the narrowest and most slippery of beams would have been safer than the loose stones and sods of turf which had lately been used by some peasants to stop up deficiencies in the footway.

The water continually rushing past made it only a question whether some of this rubbish would give way at the moment when we trusted our weight to it, or whether it would hold out a few hours longer: more than that was impossible; and the question became not only one of constant recurrence, but also of considerable importance, as the fall that must have followed a slip would have been most serious where the precipitous rocks descended for a great depth from close to our very feet. There is a better path higher up, which can, I believe, be crossed by mules; but the one we took would be rather a disagreeable matter for unsteady heads or feet.

The difficulty was of course considerably owing to the heavy rain of the night before: we passed it safely, however, and turning to the right, round the head of the kind of bay I have mentioned, we began a pleasant ascent over turf, with the highest pines dispersed gracefully about it.

This brought us out upon a higher plateau of rough wild country, intersected by a stream of spring water. At the further end was a wall-like mass of red rocks, surrounded with craggy peaks, like those which flank the parallel pass of the Gemmi; and over these I knew the Rawyl route led, though they were to all appearance inaccessible. A very remarkable jet of water bursts with considerable volume out of the rocks on the left, and another at a distance of about half a mile to the right is still larger, and shoots right out of the face of a precipice from the extremity of its subterranean channel, so as to form a very singular and interesting cascade, widely differing from any that I have seen elsewhere.

It was now one o'clock, and my guide proposed dining here, as we had the advantage of pure water,

T

and he expected the top of the pass to be too cold for resting.

After this halt we ascended the lofty barrier of rocks in front by a twisting path carried up their surface, which brought us out on the last plateau, a huge wilderness of shale and sand brought down from the neighbouring summits, without a single trace of path or footstep to mark the passage of a human creature. Here it was that Latrobe was nearly lost; and if bad weather came on, it would be difficult indeed for anyone not thoroughly acquainted with the way to extricate himself.

The last cloud, however, disappeared just before we reached this, our highest point, and suddenly exchanged the distant view of the vast mountains in the south for the more immediate presence of the Weisshorn and Wildstrubel on our right, and the Wildhorn, or Montagne Rouge, as my guide called it, which, with its magnificent glacier, flanked all the left of our position.

A bitter wind swept across this barren tract, and proved rather unpleasant, as we were heated with a long ascent: its effect was, however, counteracted by a little brandy, and we walked on for more than an hour without any greater change of level than a few undulations, with occasional beds of snow still lying between them, though the pass is not 8000 feet above the sea. Presently we descended rather a long slope of snow, and then, turning sharply to the left, round a shoulder of the mountain, in an instant the whole view was changed.

Thousands of feet below us was extended the green smiling line of the lovely Simmenthal, and my guide pointed out a few shining white spots which formed the village of Ander Lenk, now only three hours' walk from where we stood.

He was honest enough to say that I could not miss my way, and proposed therefore to return to his village instead of going on with me. We had by this time become excellent friends, and, as we parted with a cordial shake of the hands, he said he hoped that, if ever I returned to Ayent, I should be sure to inquire for the Drum-major.

From this point the path winds down the black side of the mountain, very much like that of the Gemmi, but surrounded with still finer scenery. At one part of it a waterfall, which appeared almost as lofty as the Staubbach, leapt down from above in so perpendicular a direction, that on looking upwards it appeared to come straight out of the sky; and, though the chief part of it falls into a cleft in the rocks, it was impossible to run past without receiving some of the lighter particles on my head. At the bottom of this path I came out upon some high pastures, and, a little further on, passed the end of a spur on the right, which had separated me from the proper head of the Ober Simmenthal. A magnificent cascade is very finely seen from near here, after which the whole of the valley above Oberried comes into sight; and then, if not before, I was convinced of the superiority of the Rawyl route as compared with the Gemmi.

The lofty snow-crowned Wildstrubel fills up all the head of the valley with striking grandeur, and from its gleaming side the Räzli glacier spreads itself, pouring forth a succession of cascades, which leap down in white flashing streaks over-the dark walls of rock. Full of a perfect sense of enjoyment, I walked through miles of this lovely valley, passing over rich meadows where the people were haymaking or paying an evening visit to their cattle.

Every variety of light and colour, from the emerald fields and dark pine forests to the snowy summit of the mountain, surrounded me in all the soft lustre of a summer evening. At about seven I walked into Ander Lenk, just as the white crest of the Wildstru-

... impossible to run past without ...
... the ... r particles on my h...
... of C... path I came out upon a...
... and, a little forth ... ca... passed in
... on the right, which had separat...
... r head of the Ober Simm...l ...
... ... is very finely seen from ...
... ... the whole of the valley ...
... ... into sight; and then, if not be...
... ... of the superiority of the Rawyl ...
... compared with the Gemmi.

The lofty snow-crowned Wildstrubel fills up
the head of the valley with striking grandeur, at
foot its gleaming side the Rizh glacier spread
itself, pouring forth a succession of cascades, which
leap down in wide flashing streaks over the dark
walls of rock. Full of a perfect sense of enjoyment,
I walked through miles of this lovely valley, passing
over rich meadows where the people were haymaking
or paying an evening visit to their cattle.

Every variety of light and colour, from the emerald
fields and dark pine forests to the snowy summit of
the mountain, surrounded me in all the soft lustre
of a summer evening. At about seven I walked into
Ander Leuk, just as the white crest of the Wildstru-

THE WILDSTRUBEL AND RÄZLI GLACIER.

bel concentrated upon itself the light which had been enjoyed in the now darkening valley, and shone like a vast ruby set in the dark blue of the sky. A few moments afterwards the last red tinge was gone, and the full moon, rising over the snowy edge, poured its lustre into the recesses of the valley.

CHAP. XIV.

The Ober Simmenthal.—A hospitable Landlord.—The Sieben Brunnen.—The Räzli Glacier.—Long Walk down the Valley.—Boltigen.—Erlenbach.—An importunate Voiturier.—A Race into Thun.—Farewell Sunset on the Oberland Mountains.

THE village of Ander Lenk was a picture of neatness; but, from the curiosity with which the inhabitants looked at me as I walked up to the inn, I concluded that very few strangers come here to admire it. The fact is, that though thousands pass every summer through the Lower Simmenthal by the great highway from Thun to Geneva, and at Zweisimmen are only two hours from Lenk, yet the vast majority of them never think of leaving the most beaten routes, and so lose in this instance one of the most charming spots in all Switzerland.

A great many people might not unreasonably object to the difficulty of the twelve hours' journey across the Rawyl, but I cannot recommend them too strongly to leave their baggage at Zweisimmen, and take a carriage for the day to Ander Lenk, whence they can explore the head of the upper valley, and return in the evening.

I was the only visitor at the inn, and was received by the simple landlord with the greatest possible attention. He showed me into a bedroom hung with the whitest of furniture, and ornamented with most eccentric pictures of the Saints, where he left me to enjoy the view from the window, while supper was being prepared. I was still lost in admiration of the moon-lit scene when the old fellow returned, and in a rough kindly way said, I must come down and eat. His wife had made a capital plain supper, but in spite even of the best intentions I found it very difficult to eat enough to satisfy my host, who insisted on stuffing me.

When the feast was over, I invited him to come and smoke a pipe with me at the window, and I sat watching the stars come out one by one, and listening to all his enthusiastic descriptions of the beauties of his own valley, and the wonders of the Wildstrubel, until quite late enough at night for a man who had been stirring at five in the morning. I went to bed by the light of the moon, which so completely filled the room, that I was obliged to draw the curtains close before I could sleep.

My mind was made up to spend the next day in the valley, and early in the morning I found the host with breakfast ready, after which he volunteered to escort me as far as Oberried, near which he had some business to attend to. We walked together for several miles between meadows, all sparkling with the heavy dew which, after one fine day, betokens another, by the side of a pretty stream, whose banks were in many places overhung with berberry bushes laden with their crimson festoons of fruit.

At Oberried, I insisted upon my companion going no farther, as I knew he had other occupation, so I walked on by myself till I met a merry-looking little man with a scythe on his shoulder, who accosted me in pretty good French. I found he was ready to leave his work in the hayfields, and show me the way to the Sieben Brunnen, or any other point in the neighbourhood, for anything I might please to give him. I waited a little while he went to put up his scythe, and sat down to sketch a châlet, but was soon surrounded by an inquisitive group of peasants. First came a fine tall man who left his work, and sat down by my side with a very free-and-easy air, accompanied by two little children:

these were soon sent off to a field to fetch the mother, who, I suppose, was not to be deprived of an opportunity of indulging her curiosity: with her came three or four more haymakers, who had all some question to ask me with respect to my occupation and intentions. Simple, kind-hearted creatures, they all seemed to be, and when my guide rejoined me, I was endeavouring to answer questions about England and the other side of the Rawyl, about both of which they were equally in the dark.

My new guide started off with me, after all the party had insisted on shaking my hand. We followed the course of the stream up towards its head, under the Räzli glacier, and found it tumbling and bounding along in a most lively manner, sometimes rushing through a deep gorge, and wasting its fury upon rocks and stems of dead pines, and then turning the machinery of a saw-mill, obedient to the skill and energy of man. At last, however, we were led into an impenetrable mass of underwood on its right bank; and, being thus compelled to change our line of march, we moved off a little to the left, and ascending by a remarkably pretty path through woods, we arrived on a kind of plateau of high pasture, furnished with a cheese-châlet, a little beyond which we found ourselves on the edge of the stream, just where it is reunited after passing the Sieben Brunnen.

They are thus called the Seven Fountains, because until lately they distinctly consisted of that number, though they have since become more confused. The water, which is produced from the meltings of the Räzli glacier and part of the Wildstrubel snows, after descending the rocks for a great depth, crosses for a short distance over some comparatively level ground, just above the Seven Fountains, whence it issues from under the shade of trees and bushes in a great number of elegant jets, kept apart by the intervening piles of rock, and dashing down over a rough wall of about forty feet high, again unites into the stream which flows towards Oberried.

In ordinary weather the body of water is not large, but the principal attraction of the spot lies in its charming situation, and the singular manner in which so many delicate streams rush out from among the roots of trees, which conceal their previous course, and, leaping out of the cool shade, dash down towards the valley.

I took a hasty sketch of their position, but a cold wind, brought down with the falls, prevented our making a long stay close to them, heated as we were with the walk up from Oberried. We moved off to the châlet, which had been passed previously, and were invited by the owner to walk in and have something to eat: the place was rough in the extreme, but we had some capital cheese and milk, after which the good woman of the house insisted on our taking a pinch of her snuff. In exchange for this attention I gave her lord a little of my Sardinian tobacco, which he pronounced to be " sehr stark," or very strong, though he seemed to enjoy it most completely. Leaving their hut, we found a way to scramble up a considerable distance on the right, whence we had a better view of the glacier; and by this route, if we had started early, and devoted a day to it, we could have arrived at the upper part of the Wildstrubel and its glacier; a most interesting expedition it would have been, but I was obliged to abandon it for the present, as I had no more days to spare.

After a delightful ramble we again reached the valley at Oberried, where I left my companion greatly delighted with a present of two francs and a half. On arriving at the Ander Lenk inn, I found my old friend the landlord highly interested in, and delighted by, the success of my excursion; and his enthusiasm passed all bounds when I told him, with all sincerity, that I had not known what Switzerland was till I had seen the Simmenthal.

Some routes are dull in themselves; and far more, though exquisitely beautiful, are too hackneyed for the inhabitants to escape corruption; but in the line of this "happy valley" from Zweisimmen to the Rawyl, there is a rare combination of beautiful and varied scenery, with a complete simplicity of rural manners.

The sunset and moonrise were as perfect as on the evening of my arrival; but a slight frost in the morning gave the haymakers a palpable hint that the productive season was drawing to a close. I felt thoroughly sorry to part with my friend the landlord, and could hardly bring myself to ask for my bill. When I did so, he produced a slate, and setting down all the items very slowly, in figures at least an inch long, he made out a total of only nine francs and a half, though I had been two nights in the house, and had been feasted with the greatest liberality. I had intended crossing by the Grimmi pass, and descending by the Diemtigen Thal to Erlenbach, but he would not listen to such a proposal. "Non, non," he repeated, with most energetic warmth, "vous ne passerez pas par ces montagnes là;" and, declaring that route to be dull and uninteresting, he amused me by almost insisting on my going by Zweisimmen and Boltigen down the lower valley, adding, that I could walk the whole way to Thun in nine hours, which last statement I was afterwards led by experience to think he would not have made, had he ever performed the distance himself on foot, as the Swiss very seldom walk more than a league in the hour.

At eight o'clock on a cloudless morning, with the fresh due glittering on the grass and hanging on the red berberries, I started down the valley at a quick pace, stopping now and then to look back at the glories of the Wildhorn and Wildstrubel till a bend in the road hid them from my view. In four hours I arrived at Boltigen, a pretty village close to the commencement of a very singular range of conical mountains, which extend nearly to the shores of the lake of Thun, the rocky peaks of which, rising out of dark forests, are so similar that it is difficult to know one of them from another.

Here I intended to stay only an hour for dinner; but, falling in with a member of my old college, I was induced to stay nearly double that time, chatting over Trinity days.

At last I started again as fast as I could, for I knew that there was a long walk before me. A return *voiturier* was very anxious to take me to Thun; but I had no wish to spoil the enjoyment of walking through this beautiful valley, and I went on, with the river rushing down on my right among woods and villages, surrounded by orchards and gardens, where pears were being shaken from the trees with long sticks, as though they were walnuts.

The neat shining village of Erlenbach, with its pretty spire, made me think of Latrobe, who passed many months there, and describes it with the truest affection. Nearly opposite to this there is a fine view of the opening to the Diemtigen Thal; and now for many a mile the giant pyramid of the green Niesen was full in front of me, concealing the view of the great Oberland mountains. More than three hours after I left Boltigen, my friend the *voiturier* overtook me, and again urged me to ride with him; but I kept to my purpose, assuring him that I should be at Thun in an hour and a half: he shook his head derisively, adding that he could hardly do it in that time with his horses and an empty carriage.

Lower down, the richly wooded hills press so closely on the river that is difficult to imagine where the road can be carried; however, it passes under the shade of thick overhanging firs and beeches, soon after leaving which, I cleared the shoulder of the

Niesen, and, rushing forward in eager expectation, in a moment I saw the whole range of well-known peaks from the Wetterhorn to the Jungfrau!

I was just in time to see every summit radiant with the full rosy flush of the departing sun. Never have I seen a more glorious sight, and thankful indeed I felt that, by changing my plans, I had been permitted once more to behold the giants of the Oberland.

A few minutes later the Blumlis Alp was added to the view, and being further to the west, it retained its colour a little longer than the others. Hastening on again, I rather surprised my *voiturier* friend by overtaking him at a roadside inn where he was drinking; and as darkness came on I quickened my pace, so that I arrived at Thun only five minutes after him, having walked nearly twenty-four miles, without stopping, in scarcely more than five hours. The whole distance from Lenk is rather more than thirteen leagues, and, though it had not occupied more than nine hours, exclusive of the stay at Boltigen, I had only accomplished it by dint of a pace which could hardly have been anticipated by my kind old landlord when he guessed at the time which would be required.

After getting rid of my thick shoes, and enjoying

a capital supper, I lounged about the gardens of the Bellevue, and saw the moon perfectly reflected on the calm bosom of the lake at my feet, and illuminating the picturesque turrets of the old town. I thought of the varied pleasures of the last two months, and that last splendid sunset on the mountains, which was a worthy and fitting *finale* for a delightful tour. I had again traversed the length and breadth of the land of beauty and of freedom, and seen its enchanting features in every varied circumstance of storm and sunshine. I had lounged in fertile valleys, and looked down from lofty summits on the glistening world of eternal snows: free as air, I had revelled in a liberty incomprehensible to those who have not made trial of it; and with a feeling of profound regret, I looked forward to the prospect of foggy winter in London.

Nothing now remained but a walk into Berne, with the Blumlis Alp smiling a farewell behind me, and a pleasant journey in the diligence to Basle; the busy city and the whirling Rhine told the tale of commerce and activity; and so, adieu to the mountains!

CHAP. XV.

Choice of a Route. — Pleasures of a Second Visit. — The Outfit. — Guides. — Remarks on Fatigue. — Tales of Suffering. — Mountain Sickness. — Want of Food. — The Land of Freedom. — Alpine Scenery in general. — To say he "did it."

In preparing for a first journey to Switzerland and the Alps of Savoy, it is of course of the greatest importance to decide upon the best route for seeing the country to advantage; and with this view I think it is to be recommended that the round of its beauties be made in such a way as to enable the traveller to see them in a gradually increasing scale. "Omne ignotum pro magnifico est" has long been an admitted axiom, but it is something of a disappointment to find, after seeing the grandest features first, that the remainder of the "unknown" is not so "magnificent" as that which has been seen already visited.

The facilities for reaching the lake of Geneva and the glories of Mont Blanc in two or three days from

London, tempt too many to start post haste for Chamonix before seeing the beautiful but less magnificent scenery of the Oberland. I am induced to think, after several summers' experience of the country, that it is a great advantage to enter it from the north, either by Basle or Schaffhausen, and of these the latter is probably preferable. Either of them, however admits of a great variety of ways for exploring the Oberland, according to the strength and inclination of the traveller.

All this forms excellent preparation for the much greater sublimity of Monte Rosa and Mont Blanc: the southern districts of Saas and Zermatt, or Chamonix, may be reached by several highly interesting passes, some of which I have attempted to describe in these pages; but it should be borne in mind, in determining which of these two regions is to have the priority, that the high elevation of the mountain home on the Riffelberg, requires, if possible, the earlier part of the season; whilst, in the more uncertain weather of September, there are far more easily accessible places to be seen in the neighbourhood of Chamonix; and if the worst comes to the worst, if the fine weather breaks up entirely, there is at all events a means of safe and speedy retreat to Geneva by the high road from the latter point.

Setting aside, therefore, all attempts to compare the claims of two classes of scenery, which, although very different, are perhaps equally magnificent, it would seem desirable, upon general grounds, to visit the neighbourhood of Monte Rosa, and, if possible, complete the tour of it, before setting out for the St. Bernard and the tour of Mont Blanc.

Having thus obtained a general idea of the country, the traveller will afterwards find his greatest delight in revisiting it, and devoting his time and attention to more carefully examining particular districts. The scale of Alpine scenery is so vast that it is scarcely possible to comprehend its grandeur and variety at a first observation; the eye cannot take in, and the memory cannot retain, more than a part of the surrounding objects; and upon repetition of the visit, they are found to be far more admirable than was at first imagined.

No small pleasure, too, is it to know that, after a considerable acquaintance with the country, there is scarcely a valley which you have once traversed, where you may not find some former guide or acquaintance among the inhabitants, ready to welcome you again to their neighbourhood with a hearty and sincere shake of the hand.

The land is "all before you, where to choose," and

so are the methods of travelling in it. There are three distinct modes of visiting Switzerland, to be respectively adopted according to the energy, powers, and ambition of the traveller. Those who either cannot, or will not, either walk or ride on horseback, may yet see a great deal without touching either a saddle or a pair of hob-nailed shoes; the next variety is for those who are willing to take a horse or mule, by means of which they may cross a great number of mountain passes, and ascend many fine points of observation; but the trackless plains of snow, the wonders of the glacier-world, and the awful crests of the High Alps, are reserved as the exclusive privilege of the pedestrian.

To the latter class more especially this volume is addressed: and to those whose aspirations are already directed to the high mountains, or who may possibly be animated by these pages to their exploration, I hope that I may take the liberty of offering a few words of advice.

First and foremost, the pedestrian must, of course, take care of his feet: the whole pleasure of a summer is often spoiled by severe blisters being raised at the first start, which, after entirely preventing walking for a week, leave the victim in a half-crippled state for some time longer. The best precaution against this vexation is to have the shoes or boots neither too tight nor too loose, with soles nearly half an inch thick, and broader than the upper leather, to protect the feet from innumerable rocks and stony places. The socks should be of the best wool, for two reasons; they are the least likely to rub the feet, and, even though wet through all day, they present no kind of discomfort. If shoes are worn, a pair of strong gaiters should always be carried in the knapsack for service in the soft snows; and though gloves may be safely rejected as a vanity for twelve hours out of thirteen, a thick strong pair will occasionally be found almost invaluable in a scramble over high ice-covered rocks. Many recommend the use of spikes, to screw into the shoes when travelling over ice; and, as I have heard of their great utility from those who are well entitled to give an opinion, I can have no doubt of it; though, for my own part, I have always found a double row of large-headed nails round the whole edge of the shoes, with a few stragglers in the middle, sufficient for all purposes, and possessing the advantage of being always ready; and there are very few villages, even among the mountains, where deficiencies in their "serried ranks" cannot be made good in a quarter of an hour.

The knapsack should be as light and comfortable as possible, consistent with its holding all absolute necessaries; and I think that those made of waterproof by Edmiston answer all the requisite conditions better than any others that I have seen. It is very commonly remarked, "Oh, but you can buy one for half the money at Basle or Zurich!" This is perfectly true, but I fancy that few who have tried the stiff machines of the country will hesitate in preferring the English manufactured article.

The most necessary item in its contents is undoubtedly a spare pair of thin trowsers, the want of which often involves the ignoble necessity of retreating to bed after a wet day's walk. Add to this an extra flannel shirt, with a few collars for full dress, a pair of patent leather Albert slippers to do duty as evening boots, a few brushes and other small miscellanies of the toilet, with gaiters, and a few pairs of socks, and handkerchiefs, and you have all that you can really want, in a small space, and not weighing more than a few pounds. A blue or green veil, to be worn in long days on the snow, should not be forgotten; and, in case no more important instruments are taken, a pocket-compass and a small thermometer will be found useful and valuable companions.

The best alpenstocks are to be found in the

neighbourhood of the Rigi, where they are made of a light but close-grained wood, which is infinitely stronger than, and superior to, the more ordinary fir; and, as a life may be almost imperilled in some places by their breaking, their selection becomes a matter of considerable importance.

I need scarcely add that, for all difficult expeditions among the high mountains, it is of the greatest consequence to choose good guides. An amateur must have the experience of many summers before he should venture on the upper snows, relying only on his own and his friend's resources. No doubt, he might often return successfully; but, in the event of very bad weather, which often comes on suddenly, he would sorely feel the want of skilful guides, who seem to have a peculiar instinct for enabling them to overcome, or get out of, grave difficulties among the mountains. Bad guides are often worse than none; but it is generally possible to hear of good ones. At Chamonix, as I have said before, the vexatious *règlement* prevents all power of selection, unless, by a little bribery, an unknown guide can be induced to change his turn with one of acknowledged reputation.

But when all precautions have been taken, it will still be found that the power of enduring continued exertion without suffering fatigue is the principal qualification for thorough enjoyment among the mountains. The most beautiful walk possible will become a "bore" when the limbs are weary; and the most charming view will scarcely compensate for the thorough depression of spirits brought on by too great a tension of the bodily powers. Except in the case of those who are constantly accustomed to active exercise, or have gone through some gradual preparatory training in minor expeditions, it is absurd to suppose that the lofty snows of Mont Blanc, or the dizzy crest of Monte Rosa, can be reached without considerable fatigue, or even suffering.

Though there is no doubt that some discomfort has been felt occasionally on the highest mountains by those who have not been without practice and experience, yet I think we may fairly account for many marvellous tales of misery endured by various persons, whilst ascending, or being dragged up, Mont Blanc, and even less lofty eminences, by supposing that all their powers of mind and body must have been deteriorated by excessive fatigue, perhaps not altogether without the aid of nervousness, incurred in attempting an expedition for which they were not, at all events at that time, entirely qualified.

How fearful some of these stories are! One man loses the power of eating, another can no longer smoke; the legs of one, and the head of another, refuse to perform their proper office, while a third is only brought to his senses by repeated applications of brandy or Eau de Cologne, if he is fortunate enough to possess any. Some bleed at the nose, mouth, and ears; some can only breathe by lying on their faces, after every three or four steps; and others express their firm conviction, that, if a pistol were fired off close to their ears, they would scarcely be able to hear it. One gentleman has gone so far as to assert that the rarefaction of the air causes a relaxation of the ligaments of the knee and hip-joints, and thereby accounts for his being no longer able to use his legs. Surely some of these symptoms may be attributed to the effect of what is popularly called "bad wind," and others to that of extreme exhaustion; for it is a somewhat singular circumstance, that none of these gentlemen whose sufferings I have read of appear to have felt the slightest inconvenience *from the very moment of their beginning to descend;* though, if their discomforts proceeded solely from rarefaction of the air, it is scarcely to be supposed that a few yards of descent would remedy the difficulty.

As far as my own experience goes, and that of several of my more immediate friends, I can have not the least hesitation in saying that we have always found the processes of eating, drinking, and smoking go on with complete satisfaction on the highest peaks that we have attained; and even on the summit of Monte Rosa, at more than 15,000 feet above the sea, our only regret was that we could not spend a whole day there instead of an hour.

I am aware that there is an opinion that a great difference must exist between the atmospheres of Mont Blanc and Monte Rosa; but this seems at variance with the fact that a select few have in the last two years ascended both these giants of the Alps without sustaining the least inconvenience upon either of them.

Surely, the truth must be, that of the many who have made the ascent of Mont Blanc, some at least must have been more or less unequal to the task, which is undeniably severe, and relied upon the strength of their party and the number of their guides for carrying them through difficulties which can only be overcome with satisfaction by the individual powers of the climber.

That which is properly called mountain-sickness is not at all peculiar to great elevations; and I have known instances of it, not only on the most insignificant cols in Switzerland, but also in the Scotch Highlands, and the mountains of Cumberland: in all the cases that I have been aware of, *want of food*, combined with wet or cold, was the chief cause of the malady. Giddiness, with symptoms of intoxication, is followed by an insuperable desire to lie down and sleep, however wet or miserable the mountain-side may be; and if there were no one at hand to prevent this, the sleep would probably be that which knows no waking. At all times, and especially in doubtful weather, it is of the greatest consequence to eat as good a breakfast as can be got before starting for a day's walk in mountain regions; and a mere crust of bread in the pocket may do important service before the close of the expedition.

Any one endowed with a fair share of strength and activity, as well as with a taste for the sublime and beautiful, will find the truest enjoyment and excitement among the wonders of the High Alps; and many who little think themselves capable of much exertion may find a surprising accession of power created by the exhilarating effects of a mountain life.

The exquisite sense of freedom, which seems to pervade the very air of Switzerland, adds no small charm to everything relating to it. No one who has roamed through its valleys or scaled its mountain-fastnesses, can fail to be impressed with the conviction, that it is, indeed, the land of liberty: and no one who has revelled in its varied charms can be surprised at the determined resolution of its inhatants that it shall remain so. They are free, because they have deserved freedom; and more than one oppressed "nationality," may with advantage take to heart the lesson declared by the difference of their fates.

The general character of the charms of Swiss scenery bears witness to the truth of that old axiom of our copy-books, " Change delights, and variety is pleasing." Not only does the whole country form an extraordinary contrast to all that we have been accustomed to, even in the most picturesque parts of our own country, but the walk or ride of each day may bring the traveller through an ever-varying course of beauty. Seated under the shade of a richly-clustered vine or wide-spreading walnut, with a bounding stream at his feet, he sees a long winding valley before him flanked by lofty hills and dark belts of wood, with its extremity terminated by some magnificent peak, like the Jungfrau or the Breithorn, rising far into the heavens and forming a surpassingly beautiful contrast between the clear white of its crown and the blue intensity of the sky.

In his progress up the valley every turn in the path discloses some fresh mountain, some dazzling glacier far above the green woods, some new scene of enchantment: and, if his inclination carries him so far, he may in four or five hours stand on one of the lofty summits which he has been admiring from below, and look down upon the inverted prospect. A few hours more, and he may find himself in a total change of scene, perhaps even among the luxuriance of the sunny Italian land.

Those whose fancy induces them to penetrate among the loftiest of the Alps, and to scale the dizzy precipices which were long considered the sacred home of the chamois, find in their adventures an exhilaration and delightful excitement which are inconceivable to those who have never done the same. Some remark quietly, "Well, I hear that there has been another fool on the top of Mont Blanc!" or, imagining that he could only have been there for the sake of saying that he had "done it," they refer him to Sheridan, who, when his son asked permission to go down into a coal-pit, avowedly for the mere pleasure of saying that he had been there, replied, "Well, then, why don't you say so?"

This, however, is, I imagine, the last idea likely to occur to a real lover of the mountains, an admirer of Nature in her grandest forms: he finds in his most difficult excursions, not merely an exciting and adventurous sport, but the enjoyment of a new sensation — that of being brought into immediate contact with the brilliant wonders of an unknown world. He must have a dull soul indeed if he does not return impressed with a sense of awful grandeur, which can never be forgotten, or adequately described. He must be less than a man, if he fails to derive some much higher gratification from his expedition than the mere pleasure of saying that he "did it."

APPENDIX

APPENDIX.

REMARKS UPON CERTAIN OBSERVATIONS WITH REGARD TO THE NATURE AND MOTION OF GLACIERS.

The whole subject of glaciers has been treated in so able and eloquent a manner by Professor J. D. Forbes, of Edinburgh, that I should have been very unwilling to do more than refer all those who are interested in the question, to his "Travels in the Alps," for complete information upon it, had not a lecture been delivered at the Royal Institution, in the month of January last, by Professor Tyndall, who attempted to throw grave doubts upon the soundness of Professor Forbes' views.

A paper of "Observations upon Glaciers" was presented to the Royal Society as the joint production of Messrs. Tyndall and Huxley; and the *Westminster Review* for April, 1857, in an article which would appear to be inspired from the same source, supports the new opinions.

Under these circumstances, it might be as well to examine what is the difference which has arisen, and what grounds there may be for it.

In the first place, Professor Forbes' observations placed beyond the possibility of doubt the facts that glaciers move, and that the ice in the centre moves faster than that which is near the sides. It appears to be equally true that the ice which is near the surface moves faster than that which is near the bed of the glacier. These phenomena are precisely what we find in the motion of a river, where the upper and central parts of the water move more rapidly than those at the sides and bottom of the stream, being less influenced by friction.

Many other properties of glaciers were established by his labours; but these are for the present sufficient to show the strength of the grounds which he had for drawing his analogy between the motion of a glacier and that of a river. After summing up the result of his observations, he deduces therefrom this theory :—" That a glacier is, in truth, a sluggish stream, moulding itself, notwithstanding the apparent hardness and fragility of the ice, over the inequalities of its bed and the irregularities of its confining banks, and retaining its coherence throughout, notwithstanding the numerous cracks by which its surface is fissured, in consequence of an inherent plasticity of its substance, which only becomes sensible under intense and long-continued pressure, producing a very slow motion."

The Westminster reviewer acknowledges the great obligations due to Professor Forbes, and does not hesitate to adopt so much of his theory as relates to the motion of a glacier. He admits that "in fact, the glacier is a river of ice, and the *névé* is its source." He goes on to say,— "What is the crackling, and rushing, and groaning, one

APPENDIX. 307

hears all day upon a glacier? It is the noise of the ice-torrent. What are the long lines of masses of rock, of all sizes, from mere splinters to huge blocks as big as a house, which one sees scattered along the flanks of the glacier, and ranged in the middle wherever two glaciers have joined into one? These are the sticks and straws which are being floated down by the ice-river."

The reviewer admits the *differential motion* of the ice which I have alluded to; he admits, also, the fact that a glacier "fits itself into dilatations of its valley, and squeezes through narrow ravines;" he admits, in short, all the river-like phenomena which Professor Forbes vindicates for a glacier; but then he will no further go.

"By a natural transition," he says, "Professor Forbes, having established that a glacier moves after the manner of a viscous body, supposes that therefore it is viscous; that it is comparable to lava, to tar, to semi-fluid plaster-of-Paris, and that it is for this reason that it flows down the inclined floor of its valley. But surely it is no very logical procedure to conclude, from the resemblance of two bodies in one particular, that they are therefore alike in all? Suppose we turn the argument another way, taking for the purpose a comparison frequently used by Professor Forbes himself. A glacier moves in the same way as the river Rhone flows, therefore it is a limpid fluid."

It would, doubtless, be quite as reasonable to say, "The Rhone flows in the same way as a glacier moves, therefore it is a *viscous* fluid." But, in fact, the fallacy of the proposition consists in the improper use of the words, "in the same way." Does the writer mean the "same way" *in all respects*, and thereby include the same *absolute velocity*, for instance? If he does, he merely seems to state the self-evident proposition, that, if two things are not in any respect different, therefore they are in all respects similar. If he does not use the words in that sense, he draws an inference which probably neither Professor Forbes, nor anyone else would assent to.

The next point to ascertain is, what are the precise grounds which induce Professor Tyndall and the reviewer to assert that Professor Forbes has drawn an illogical conclusion?

Setting aside minor points of detail, it seems that they take their stand upon the demonstrable fact that a piece of ice is brittle and cleaveable under the influence of pressure; and, therefore, they assert that a *glacier* cannot be a viscous fluid.

Now nobody was more aware of the brittleness and cleaveability of a piece of ice than Professor Forbes was when he stated his theory; and no one has mentioned this property more clearly. Like Professor Tyndall, he considers that the blue bands or veins in the ice, generally perpendicular to the direction of greatest pressure, are caused by it; but he does not consider that this fact is inconsistent with the possibility of the *mass of the glacier* being what may properly be called a viscous, or imperfect fluid.

Here, then, is the stumbling point; and at this stage, therefore, it becomes necessary to define what an imperfect or viscous fluid is; what, in fact, are the limits of fluidity?

Turning to the article on hydrostatics in the "Encyclopædia Britannica," we find that Sir Isaac Newton's definition of a fluid is, that it is "a body yielding to any force impressed, and which hath its parts very easily moved one among another."

The same article says, " Sir I. Newton held all matter to be originally homogeneous, and that from the different modification and texture of it alone, all bodies receive their various structure, composition, and form. In his definition of a fluid, he seems to imply that he thought fluids to be composed of primary solids ; and, in the beginning of his "Principia," he speaks of sand and powder as imperfect fluids."

Now, with respect to a glacier, neither party appears to have any doubt that, if a vast number of points could be marked in a plane of the ice, perpendicular to the surface and to the direction of the glacier, and extending across its entire width, after an interval of more or less time, it would be found that the points nearest to the centre of the glacier had advanced further than those at the sides; and it also appears to be generally admitted that the points near the surface of the glacier would be found to have advanced further than those in its lower portion. The evident result of this is, that what may be considered as approximately ultimate particles of the glacier, *do move among one another with different velocities.*

Without venturing to assert that this fact is in itself sufficient to bring a glacier into the category of imperfect fluids, it would nevertheless be well to consider some simple illustrations of the *possible limits of fluidity.*

Suppose a cubic yard of iron to be placed on a gentle incline, rough enough to prevent its immediate descent. If great heat could be applied to this mass, there is no doubt it would be seen to elongate itself by degrees, then to melt, and finally to descend the incline in a state, the fluidity of which it would be difficult to deny. Who will tell us at what stage of this operation rigidity ceases, and fluidity begins?

Again,—if, as Professor Forbes suggests, we take for example the case of mortar, or even road-scrapings, and suppose a quantity of such material to be poured upon the hollow of a sloping bank, the supply being maintained from above, we should have the leading *phenomena* of a glacier. If the preparation were so dry as to move with great difficulty, the similarity of motion would be more and more complete; and if there were irregularities in the surface of the bank, the mass would exhibit fissures or crevices.

A man watching the motion of this mass, and capable of comprehending the whole at a glance, would probably not hesitate to admit it to be a more or less imperfect fluid; but if we can fancy some microscopic insect, endowed with reasoning powers, to be walking over it, and perhaps tumbling into one of the fissures, the atomy might say, "I see nothing but a quantity of damp stones and rocks. This is clearly not a viscous fluid, like the treacle in which I was once entangled." The man would consider the mass in its entirety: the observations of the insect would be confined to its ultimate particles.

The interesting experiments which were exhibited at

the Royal Institution by Professor Tyndall, to prove that portions of hard ice may be broken to powder by compression, and made to assume other forms by means of the process of regelation, may perhaps be not unfairly considered as merely experiments upon the *ultimate particles of a glacier*, proving no more as to the nature of the entire glacier than a demonstration of the rigidity of one of the ultimate particles of the mortar would prove its entire mass to be absolutely solid.

The fact is shown to be established that the particles of the glacier do, in truth, move among one another with differential velocity: the more or less "easily," of the definition before referred to, must be a mere question of degree. Great duration of time, and great pressure of gravitation have to be taken into account; and may it not fairly be considered that the individual motion of the particles of ice, whether by a process of disrupture and regelation, or otherwise, is a matter wholly underlying and subordinate to the main question of the nature and motion of a glacier?

If the fact that the particles composing a glacier move among one another with a continued differential motion, under the pressure of gravity and of the superincumbent mass of its upper regions, *without any extraneous force*, be not sufficient to bring such a mass under a true definition of an imperfect fluid, will the objectors give us such a definition as will exclude it? If a glacier be excluded from the list of fluids more or less imperfect, may we not, perhaps, hesitate to include among them such substances as lava, tar, treacle, or even the Thames at low tide?

Failing some such strict definition, may it not fairly be assumed that a glacier, in the aggregate, exhibiting, as it has been proved to do, the general phenomena of a viscous or imperfect fluid, is in fact such a fluid, notwithstanding any prejudices to the contrary which may be caused by the brittleness of its parts?

At all events, without a clear definition of the ultimate limits of imperfect fluidity, it seems scarcely logical to attempt to show that Professor Forbes' theory is opposed to a true view of the question.

THE END.

London:
Printed by Spottiswoode & Co.
New-street Square.

Lightning Source UK Ltd.
Milton Keynes UK
UKHW022239220119
336029UK00009B/734/P